John Bradley, John A Lawson

A narrative of travel and sport in Burmah, Siam and the Malay Peninsula

John Bradley, John A Lawson

A narrative of travel and sport in Burmah, Siam and the Malay Peninsula

ISBN/EAN: 9783742891433

Manufactured in Europe, USA, Canada, Australia, Japa

Cover: Foto ©Andreas Hilbeck / pixelio.de

Manufactured and distributed by brebook publishing software (www.brebook.com)

John Bradley, John A Lawson

A narrative of travel and sport in Burmah, Siam and the Malay Peninsula

A NARRATIVE

OF

TRAVEL AND SPORT

IN BURMAH, SIAM, AND THE MALAY
PENINSULA.

BY

JOHN BRADLEY,

London:
SAMUEL TINSLEY,
10, SOUTHAMPTON STREET, STRAND.
1876.
(*All Rights reserved.*)

CONTENTS.

CHAPTER I.

Introductory observations—Difficulty in obtaining companions for the journey—Start for Rangoon—Meet with Captain Lacy and Mr. Grant—Arrangements for the journey—Price of horses at Rangoon—The expedition organized by Mr. Grant—Our outfit and stores—Burmese oxen—Start for Pegu—The road between Rangoon and Pegu—Arrival at Pegu—Description of the city—Temple of Shoomadoo—Ruins in the neighbourhood of Pegu—The Sittang road—Bengalee road-surveyor—Tadenbah—Hospitality of the natives—Banks of the Sittang—Pretty appearance of the city—Manufactories at Sittang—Ferried across the river—Streets of Sittang—The bazaar—Long marches exhaust the oxen—A Burmese house -   - Page 1

CHAPTER II.

Description of the country near Sittang—Plantations of rice, &c.—Buddhist priest—Patandah—An evening's shooting—Extraordinary sagacity of an elephant—Streams—Wild country—The Salween—Difficulty in crossing—Shallangat—Preparations for sport—Forest and jungle—In the jaws of a tiger—Extent of my injuries—Kindness of a native woman—Several tigers shot by my companions—A native clawed—Destruction of human life by wild beasts—Trophies of the chase—Resume our journey—Difficulties of travelling in the forest—Rate of progress—Deer shot - - - - - - - 25

CHAPTER III.

Party of natives and their village—Paucity of large game met with—Rough ground—Wild elephants—One of them shot—Elephants' feet not a dainty—The river Thungyen—Cobras and green snakes—Our servants lost—A night out and its drawbacks—Wild beasts and their fondness for water—Captain Lacy goes in search of the men—The baggage arrives—The passage of the river—A day's rest—Results of an evening's shooting—Impenetrable forests compel us to make detours—Change in the character of the country—Plains covered with beautiful flowers—Average distance an ox can travel—Arrive at a large village—Surrounded by the crowd—A native girl seized by a tiger—Number of natives killed by tigers - 47

CHAPTER IV.

Traces of the accident—Preparations for the destruction of the tiger—Remains of the victim—Unsuccessful search—A deserted village—A leopard shot—Captain Lacy's account of his adventure with a tiger—A native badly hurt—Return to Sattybardah—Offer a reward for the discovery of the man-eater's lair—Evidences of its dreadfully destructive powers—Prepare to meet our antagonist — A double adventure — Marvellous tenacity of life—Excitement at Sattybardah on the news of our success — Size and weight of the tigers—Large bag of game made on the 4th December—Indian bird of paradise—Bees—Parrots—Villages—Tormented by mosquitos Page 69

CHAPTER V.

Our position—Monotonous rustling of the leaves—Signs of inhabitants—Flat country—Rhinoceroses—Fruit—Pagodas and priests—Civil disposition of the natives—Siamese cities—Sahaing—Large number of tame elephants seen in the streets—The city nuisances— Anecdotes of hawks — Cock-fighting—Curious soap-stone ornaments—Strange tricks of a travelling conjuror—Pleasure evinced by the crowd—Annoying insects and lizards, and nightmare - - - - 91

CHAPTER VI.

Hot day—River Menam—Parties of natives met—Dense forest—Pea-fowl shooting—An aquatic village—Marshy ground—A tiger shot—Two buffaloes shot—A sporting expedition—Inundated tracts of country—Numerous traces of game—A herd of large deer—Magnificent banyan tree—A solitary rhinoceros seen, and shortly afterwards others found—One of them placed *hors de combat*—Damage done to crops by rhinoceroses and other wild beasts — Cowardice displayed by tigers—Several shot by ourselves and servants—Magnificent display of fire-flies—These insects preyed upon by a small kind of hawk—Boggy nature of the country—Excessive heat - 109

CHAPTER VII.

Pace of the oxen—Range of hills—Character of the country—Monkeys, and a free-fight amongst them—Wild bees' nests—Ruins of a pagoda—Wells—Storms of hail and rain—Trees found in this region—Stream and lotus flowers—Cultivated land—Village or town of Tatsong—Rajah of Tatsong—Description of the place—The Rajah's palace—Courteous reception by the Rajah—His personal appearance—Subjects of our conversation—His territory—A tiger hunt proposed—In the howdah—The sport commences—Timidity of the beaters—Character of the tiger—A desperate encounter—A native saved by his elephant—Result of our day's sport - - - 129

CHAPTER VIII.

Dinner at the Rajah's palace—His Highness elated—Elephant stables—White elephant—Trade of the country—Productions—Elephant hunting—Christmas Day—An elephant hunt—Its failure—A second expedition—Exciting adventure with a large male elephant—Terror of the herd—Cruelty of the Rajah—Affecting tenderness of an elephant dam for its calf—Long march of the beaters and servants—A day's rest—The Rajah offended—Leave Tatsong—Three villages seen—People at work—Four large brooks—Snipe—Very large bag made   Page 157

CHAPTER IX.

Regain banks of the Menam—Rate of progress—Gigantic forests—Height of the trees—Appearance of the river—Flamingoes—Frilled lizards—Marshy ground—Alligators and tigers—Disturbed by the noise of wild beasts—Fight between a bull-buffalo and a rhinoceros—Extraordinary display of fire-flies—Tigers and buffalo—Cross a tributary of the Menam—Flying squirrels—Dangerous marshy ground — Loss of an ox and narrow escape of Mr. Grant—Miserable plight—Another ox lost—Desperate situation—Apathy of our servants—Strange appearance of the trees—Illness of Mr. Grant—He and a servant attacked by fever—Weed of which cattle are fond—Continued illness of Mr. Grant   -   -   -   177

CHAPTER X.

Improvement in Mr. Grant's condition—Beautiful little finch—Resume our journey—Small plains—Sharp encounter with a rhinoceros—A rhinoceros killed with a single shot—Boats and rafts pass down the river—Reeds, mosquitos and gnats—Extraordinary appearance of the clouds—The forest appears to be a mass of silvery light—Description of the country—Find remains of a buffalo—A tiger shot—Dense forest—Compelled to camp out—Men sent in search of us   -   -   197

CHAPTER XI.

Village in an unusually filthy state—Inquisitiveness of the natives—Fruit abundant—Density of the population—Large tracts cleared of timber—Horrors of a night in a native hut—Enormous number of rats—Compelled to turn out—Differences with our landlord—Large river—Slaughter of buffaloes—Fauna met with—Domestic animals — Ferocious dog—Tedious march—Arrive at Siam—Disposition of the natives—Siamese dramatic entertainment—Extensive rice fields—Pretty scenery—Arrival at Bangkok—Meet with an Englishman, and are kindly entertained by him—Floating houses—Alteration of our arrangements—Mr. Grant leaves for Rangoon   -   -   217

CHAPTER XII.

Preparations for our expedition to Malaya—Sail for Patani—The ship's crew—Duration of our voyage—Patani and its inhabitants—We land—Character of the country—Pass a night in a native hut—Villages and cultivated ground—Singular appearance of the forest—Large snake—Wasp-like fly—Gloom of the forest—Rivulet—Slow rate of progress—Exceedingly dense forest—Rest and sleep—Our discomforts   -   241

CHAPTER XIII.

Continuation of our journey through dense forests—Gigantic fungi—Snakes—Birds' nests—Exclusion of the sun's rays from these forests—Our progress southwards—Pass the night in a hollow tree—Terrific storm—Vividness of the lightning—The two Chinamen leave us—Their probable fate—Suffer from thirst—Pleasing circumstances—Springs and pools of water—Little change in the character of the forest—Dine off serpent's flesh—Increased difficulties of our journey—High trees and monkeys—Reduced to eat small birds—Elephant shot—Beneficial effects of the excitement - - - Page 259

CHAPTER XIV.

The forest less dense—A herd of elephants seen—Longer march than usual—Small pool of water—Two deer obtained—Our view of the surrounding country limited—Handsome parrot—Trees met with here—Spring—Tiring detours—Our bed—Decide to make for Province Wellesley—Chain of mountains in sight—Flights of birds going southwards—Halt on summit of hills—Discovery of tree-huts of wild men—Thorn creepers—Wild men—Their appearance and manners—A girl captured—The tree-huts—Articles found in them—Description of our captive—Small river—Deer and antelope shot—Guard kept during the night - - - - - 283

CHAPTER XV.

Our captive's appetite—Succeed in communicating with the wild men—Their degraded state and morals—Numbers—Mode of procuring fire—Resume our journey—Our captive anxious to go with us—Proceed up the river—More dense forests—A white peacock—Appearance of the range—Pool or lake—Find a couple of tapirs, and shoot one—Description of the animal—Valleys with pools—More tree-huts, and traces of supposed cannibalism—Country difficult of access—Another colony of wild men—Find it impossible to communicate with them 305

CHAPTER XVI.

Commence ascent of the mountains—Sides very steep and covered with forests—Gamboge and pine trees—Growth of the trees—Our highest point—Pigeons—Dark night—Sublime Scene—Descend on the west side of the range—Height of the thermometer — Fearful storm — Quantity of game — Discover a party of natives—Their weapons—A nearly white tapir shot—Use of the proboscis—Hilly district—Retarded by denseness of the forest—Follow the course of a stream—A large python—Description of the river—Reach the sea-shore—Purchase a prah at a Malay hamlet and embark for Penang—Arrive at Georgetown—Conclusion - - - - 323

A NARRATIVE
OF
TRAVEL AND SPORT.

CHAPTER I.

Introductory observations.—Difficulty in obtaining companions for the journey.—Start for Rangoon.—Meet with Captain Lacy and Mr. Grant.—Arrangements for the journey.—Price of horses at Rangoon.—The expedition organized by Mr. Grant.—Our outfit and stores.—Burmese oxen.—Start for Pegu.—The road between Rangoon and Pegu.—Arrival at Pegu.—Description of the city.—Temple of Shoomadoo.—Ruins in the neighbourhood of Pegu.—The Sittang road.—Bengalee road-surveyor. — Tadenbah. — Hospitality of the natives.—Banks of the Sittang.—Pretty appearance of the city.—Manufactories at Sittang.—Ferried across the river.—Streets of Sittang.—The bazaar.—Long marches exhaust the oxen.—A Burmese house.

TRAVELLERS and explorers may be divided, I think, into two great classes: those whose chief object is the attainment of scientific information, and those who travel principally for the gratification of their love of adventure and change of scenery. I belong to the latter section, and I have an innate love of wandering in countries which are but little known and frequented by Europeans. This is probably one of the reasons why I have generally found it difficult to persuade any of my countrymen to accompany me in my travels. Indian sportsmen can usually find plenty of game in the neighbourhood of the cantonments, and it is not often that they undertake a long and dangerous journey for the sole purpose of shooting tigers and deer. Some Anglo-Indians, indeed, are fond of long rambles in search of game; but they almost invariably choose those tracts of the country which are best known, and where travelling is comparatively safe and easy. And so it happened, that when I first formed the idea of penetrating into the interior of Siam, and working my way down towards the Malay Peninsula, I could not induce any of my Indian friends and acquaintances to join me in the expedition, or even to countenance and encourage the proposed undertaking; and I was compelled to leave Calcutta for Rangoon, the point from whence I proposed to start, alone.

At Rangoon, however, good fortune awaited me. I was there introduced to a Captain Lacy, who had formerly been an officer of the Bengal Native Infantry. He was an enthusiastic sportsman, and readily fell in with my views and intentions; and he also prevailed upon a young friend of his, Mr. Grant, to make one of our party. The arrangements for the journey were that we should penetrate into the kingdom of Siam, by way of Pegu and Sittang, and thence work our way down to Bangkok. I had an intention of extending my travels into some parts of the Malayan Peninsula, but I could not get my companions to promise to go farther than Bangkok, from which city they hoped to be able to return to India by water. We agreed to perform the journey leisurely, and along our route to enjoy tiger-shooting and other sports, as circumstances might permit. A number of native servants were hired, and pack-oxen purchased to carry our baggage. Part of the men were especially engaged as personal servants to myself and companions, and were trained men who had been in the employ of European residents; the remainder, six in number, were Burmese, intended to look after the oxen. These latter men were procured for the very moderate remuneration of eight rupees a month per man. The number of pack-oxen provided for our expedition was eight, all fine strong animals.

After making inquiries, Captain Lacy, Mr. Grant, and myself came to the conclusion that we should not meet with any impediment to performing the journey on horseback; and, accordingly, three horses were bought for our own use. Horses were scarce at Rangoon, but we succeeded in obtaining three passable, though small, mares, for an average sum of three hundred and forty rupees a head.

The trouble of organizing our little party, and making the necessary preparations, fell almost entirely upon Mr. Grant, who entered heartily into the business; and it is impossible to say how much the success of our undertaking was indebted to the care and discrimination he exercised in selecting the servants, who all turned out to be faithful and trustworthy men. It was through his forethought also that we were provided with a portable cooking apparatus, net-work bedsteads, and other exceedingly useful articles. Amongst the other necessaries provided may be enumerated a light field-tent, capable of comfortably accommodating the three of us, a large quantity of preserved meats, &c., spirits, drugs, water-proof blankets; and, in fact, everything that could be thought of as likely to conduce to our comfort and preserve health. These articles were packed in canvas bags, and carried upon the backs of the oxen. As the quantity of gunpowder we had with us was considerable, one beast was kept apart to carry it, in order to prevent accidents. I should state that in the province of Pegu, and other parts of India, oxen are largely used as beasts of burden by those who cannot afford to keep elephants, and are trained to the work and are very docile. Those that we bought cost us from twenty to thirty rupees each; and, though rather slow in their pace, they would cover a long distance in the course of a day.

Everything being in readiness, and our final arrangements completed, the servants and oxen, with the baggage, were sent on to Pegu, in charge of Akbar Nanee, Captain Lacy's Hindostanee servant, there to await our arrival. This was on the 8th of October, 1869, and on the morning of the 10th we left Rangoon ourselves.

The distance of Pegu from Rangoon is nearly sixty miles, and there is a tolerably good road running between the two cities. The country is exceedingly fertile, well watered, and, near Rangoon, in a high state of cultivation. Many streams and rivers run across the road, and most of them are spanned by strong bridges, though we were compelled to ford some of the shallowest of them. The number of villages and towns we passed on the road was considerable, and afforded us convenient opportunities of halting for a rest. At many places on or near the side of the road we saw great mounds of earth and stones, on the top of which sticks were planted, with coloured rags fluttering from them. Captain Lacy said he had been informed that these mounds marked the spots where persons had been seized by tigers. We had been told at Rangoon that certain parts of the road were dangerous for foot-passengers, owing to the number of tigers which infested the uncultivated tracts of country.

. Having spent the middle part of the day at a small town about fifteen miles distant from Pegu, we resumed our journey early in the evening, and arrived at the latter city a little before eight o'clock. We found our servants and the oxen established in a kind of caravansera, without the ruined walls, which is intended for the use of travellers, who pay a trifle for the accommodation. Small sheds were erected round the walls of this enclosure, for the shelter of man and beast; but, as they were far from being clean, we erected our own tent, and picketed the oxen and horses in the open square, lest standing in the mire of the sheds should give them sore feet.

The city of Pegu is situated on the left bank of a tributary of the river Sittang. It is a very ancient and partially-decayed place, and most of the city walls, together with a great many fine buildings, are in ruins. It is said the city has been gradually falling to ruin since it was captured and sacked, in the year 1757, by the Burmese Emperor Alompra, who murdered or made slaves of all the inhabitants who were unable to save themselves by a timely flight. Most of the houses, like those at Rangoon, are built upon piles, to elevate them above the level of the floods, which frequently occur. Many of the streets are narrow and crooked, and the houses bulge over them to such an extent that they appear to be about to topple down. It is a noisy and bustling place, and a considerable amount of business seems to be transacted in the bazaar, where all sorts of European and native wares are offered for sale.

But the greatest sight at Pegu is the pagodas. The day after our arrival we went to see one of the most noteworthy, called the Temple of Shoomadoo. It is a large and certainly a magnificent building, erected in the usual square Indian style of architecture. It might almost be taken for a city in itself, so great is the number of its domes, minarets, courts, and corridors. There are many signs of great antiquity about it, but it is in a good state of preservation, being well looked after by a large body of Buddhist priests, who guard the gates somewhat jealously till the would-be inspector of the interior produces a silver key. A rupee or two gained us admittance to what I suppose was the chief idol house. It was a large dimly-lighted place, about a hundred and twenty feet long, by eighty broad, as nearly as I could judge. At the farthest end from the doorway was arranged a large collection of idols of all sorts of sizes and shapes, and of every degree of hideousness. One gigantic figure, of more than satanic ugliness, was encrusted with precious stones; and there were traces about it that many of the gems had been picked out—probably by backsliding Buddhists, as I can scarcely think a European would have the opportunity of committing the theft.

OCT. 12.—We left Pegu early this morning, passing through the city, and out by the ruins of a splendid gateway on the east side. The walls near this gate were still standing, though in a dangerously ruinous condition, and were of great height, and built of immense blocks of a granite-like stone. For several miles on our way we met with ruins of various kinds, and at one spot, where a number of carved images lay about in confusion amongst scattered fragments of masonry, I was reminded vividly of some picture I have seen of ruins in the Holy Land. About an hour after leaving Pegu we came to a stream of water spanned by a well-constructed bridge, the materials for building which had evidently been furnished from amongst the ruins in the neighbourhood.

The Sittang road, upon which we were now travelling, is a good, broad, and level highway, kept in excellent repair by the natives, who have dug a ditch on either side for drainage.

For several miles beyond Pegu the land on either side of the road was under culture, the principal crop being rice; and these rice-fields were flooded artificially with water, obtained by diverting the courses of several small streams of the Sittang delta. The number of natives at work in the fields, and the many children seen in the villages we passed on our route, showed that this part of the country is pretty thickly peopled. In nearly every village we came to women were sitting on the ground under the shade of the trees, and grinding corn in the manner so universally prevalent in all eastern countries, viz., by rubbing it between two hand mill-stones. Both women and children appeared greatly astonished as we rode by them, and in some instances scrambled out of our way in manifest fright.

After passing through several tracts of forest, one of which was four or five miles in extent, we came upon a party of labourers repairing the road. They were in charge of a native of Bengal, who informed Captain Lacy that the country ahead was nearly destitute of inhabitants, but that there was a large village about two hours' journey farther on, called Tadenbah. Its distance from Pegu would be about fifteen miles, and as this was as far as we could expect the oxen to go in one day, we determined to proceed thither and await their arrival; for they had been left on the road, with all the men, to follow at their leisure. With regard to the road-surveyor, he told us that he had formerly had employment under the British Government in the Bengal Presidency, and had been in his present situation for nearly eight years. He was an intelligent and obliging man, and gave us some useful little bits of information about the country, and we all three felt pleasure in having met with him. I may mention, by the way, that the labourers fetch stone, gravel, &c., &c., from any land where it is to be found without reference to the owner or person laying claim to the said land. For the purpose of conveying the materials to the spot where they are required, they are provided with bullock-carts.

A little before eight o'clock we arrived at Tadenbah, a village consisting of sixty or eighty huts and houses built of wood, and boasting the possession of a small temple. A good stream of water ran through its midst, and the surrounding country, with the exception of a few rice-fields, was covered with fine forest trees. Our advent caused some commotion amongst the inhabitants; but the crowd which assembled was orderly though somewhat noisy. When we had dismounted and fastened our horses under a tree, several of the natives beckoned to us and pointed to the huts. We accepted the invitation, and entering one of the largest dwellings, were provided with a large wooden dish full of boiled rice and a bowl of milk each, for which, of course, we did not forget to tender payment, which was received with evident gratification. Nor did these hospitable Peguans forget to provide for our horses, for a party of boys pulled up and brought them a supply of grass. Akbar Nanee and the rest of the servants with the baggage, came up early in the afternoon; and having seen the tent pitched and preparations made for passing the night, we devoted the remainder of the day to shooting, but found no game with the exception of a few birds.

As the weather was no warmer than it usually is in England in summer, we did not start from Tadenbah the next morning until after seven o'clock. Most of the inhabitants turned out to see us off, and a few followed us a short distance along the road. Sittang was to be our halting-place to-day; and, leaving the baggage train (as usual) to follow at their lazy pace, we pushed forward more rapidly, and in half an hour struck the river Sittang, along the right bank of which the road ran. The vegetation was here exceedingly luxuriant, the gigantic trees stretching their huge limbs far over the road and river, and forming a lofty archway overhead, where thousands of gaudy and beautifully variegated parrots fluttered, their magnificent plumage rendered intensely and indescribably brilliant by the glaring rays of the sun. Many pretty lizards and other reptiles frequently ran across the road, and one or two alligators were seen in the river. The latter creatures we afterwards heard are very abundant in some parts of the Sittang.

Between nine and ten o'clock we came within sight of the domes and minarets of the city of Sittang, and a prettier scene it would be difficult to conceive. Unfortunately I am at a loss how adequately to describe the glorious scene that met our view. The reader must imagine a noble forest of immense trees, whose feathery foliage was of a hundred different shades of green, tinged with brown, and finely relieved here and there by some shrubs or small trees, bearing a deep red leaf. From amidst this splendid foliage peeped thousands of handsome little minarets and spires, some of a spiral shape, others so ornamented and perforated that they looked like delicate lace-work; and all glittering so brightly in the sun that the eyes were almost dazzled with their brilliancy. Large domes were partially visible, covered with gilt, and fantastically ornamented with curious carved devices. Nearer the river the houses were in view, built upon piles to raise them above the floods which inundate the country during the rainy season. The river itself was covered with boats, large and small, many of them serving as dwellings for their owners, who pass most of their existence on the water. When, however, they feel inclined to sojourn for a time on shore, the boat is pulled up to a dry spot and turned bottom up, one side being so propped up that the boatman and his family can easily creep under for shelter when necessary, or for the purpose of sleeping.

With the exception of a very few houses and sheds, used for manufacturing purposes, the city of Sittang is built upon the left bank of the river, about fifteen or twenty miles from its mouth. Fully one half of its inhabitants are Chinese, Anamese, Laos, and other foreigners from the neighbouring provinces and countries, who are principally engaged in the manufactures carried on at Sittang, which are not extensive, and consist of weaving linen and cotton goods, carving fancy trinkets in ivory and ornamental woods, and making the rude implements used in their agriculture. There is also a rope manufactory, where ropes and twine are made from vegetable fibre, several tan-yards and a few other factories; but none of these establishments seem to do a very flourishing business, and their trade is confined to the native population of the district.

When we had got abreast of the city we motioned to the astonished boatmen, who happened to be at hand, that we wished to be ferried over to the opposite bank. A score of boats immediately pulled up to the spot where we were standing, and the men began to quarrel vehemently which should have the privilege of taking us across, shouting and swearing in a nearly deafening tone. With much difficulty, and at the risk of being pushed into the water by the fractious ferrymen, we succeeded in getting on board — myself and

Captain Lacy, with our horses, in one boat, and Mr. Grant and his horse in another. In this fashion we were sculled across to the city, an operation which took a quarter of an hour or twenty minutes, the river being of considerable breadth at this point.

On the opposite shore some hundreds of persons witnessed our landing ; but they did not attempt to crowd round us or follow us into the city, where we did not excite as much curiosity as I had anticipated. We were permitted to ride through the street without attracting any unpleasant attention ; but a crowd of half-naked children followed close at our horses' heels. The streets were narrow, sometimes so much so that we were even compelled to ride in file, and pervaded with a shocking stench arising from the heaps of filth which lay festering in the sun. The houses were mostly built of wood, and, as at Pegu and Rangoon, elevated some distance from the ground on wooden piles, and a few on solid blocks of masonry. Access to them was gained by flights of steps, or bamboo ladders. There were many large buildings near the centre of the city, and the temples were fine specimens of Hindoo architecture; but the whole appearance of the place was so dingy, and the filthiness of it so disgusting, that I wondered it should have looked so beautiful from a distance.

The bazaar offered a singular contrast to the rest of the city. It was situated in a large square, with buildings several stories high on three sides of it, and the bustle, activity, and noise of the hundreds of persons present was quite exciting. All sorts of wares were exposed for sale, muskets, pistols, swords, daggers, knives, native bags, ivory snuff-boxes (at least they appeared to be such), scissors, needles, and bodkins, of European make; coloured feathers, jewellery, of native make; muslins, calicoes, prints, scarves, &c., both native and European; inlaid articles, fireworks, boots, sandals, turbans, and a variety of Chinese manufactures, such as hardware, fans, flowered silks, and pictures painted on rice-paper. At one part of the bazaar was a regular rag-fair. Amongst the curiosities we observed here was a number of old scarlet jackets, formerly belonging to the 28th, 50th, and 16th Native Infantry, and the 10th and 98th European Regiments; and also the jacket of some hussar regiment, and the light-blue tunic of a native cavalry soldier. These cast-off old uniforms must have gone through some strange adventures before finding themselves exposed for sale in this out-of-the-way place. It is astonishing how fond the natives of the East are of military finery. A worn-out old jacket, or a forage cap, is worth a Jew's eye to a native in any part of Hindostan and Farther India.

Making our way out of the city on the east side, we picketed our horses under a grove of palm-trees, and partook of the refreshments we had brought in our haversacks. In the course of the afternoon Mr. Grant and myself, leaving Captain Lacy to look after the horses, passed through the city on foot, and re-crossed the river to conduct the servants to our halting-place. We waited about till evening, and as they did not come up we naturally began to feel alarmed on their account, and walked a mile or two on the road to meet them. It was nearly seven o'clock before they came in sight, and the oxen were in a very distressed condition. The marches had evidently been too long for them. We soon had three of the largest ferryboats at our service; but a great deal of trouble was experienced in getting the oxen on board, and it was nearly nine o'clock before we had re-crossed the river a mile below the city; and we were here almost immediately joined by Captain Lacy, who had become much disturbed by our prolonged absence. During the night one of the poor beasts died, and we resolved that in future we would advance by shorter stages: and thinking, moreover, that our oxen might be a little too heavily burdened, we went in the morning, accompanied by one of our servants as interpreter, to purchase three others to replace our loss. We had no difficulty in procuring much finer beasts than those we already possessed.

After a consultation, we determined to spend a couple of days at Sittang, and Angbang, the interpreter alluded to above, was sent into the city with Captain Lacy's servant, Akbar Nanee, to endeavour to procure us a house. He succeeded in renting two rooms and some outhouses for the cattle, at the modest rate of two rupees per diem. These lodgings were situated in a garden, about a quarter of a mile from the city, and our landlord was a Burmese leather merchant. The two rooms occupied the lower story of the house, and each of them was about twenty feet square, without windows or any opening save the doors, and entirely destitute of anything like furniture, which had, perhaps, been removed to make way for us. A dozen roughly-constructed steps led to our basement, and above, in what I suppose were the garrets of the establishment, was located the master of the house and his family. As the floors were made of split bamboos, which bent easily under the weight of a body, we could tell by the movements overhead that there was a considerable number of persons billeted there. In fact, our quarters, though tolerably convenient, were not retired enough to be pleasant; and at night the noise and chattering overhead was a complete nuisance. Neither was the place free from insectile pests.

One room was kept to ourselves, the other was devoted to the use of the servants. Cooking and other domestic operations were carried on in a courtyard at the back of the house, where there was a well of excellent spring-water.

CHAPTER II.

Description of the country near Sittang.—Plantations of rice, &c.—Buddhist priest.—Patandah.—An evening's shooting.—Extraordinary sagacity of an elephant.—Anecdote of another elephant.—Streams.—Wild country.—The Salween.—Difficulty in crossing.—Shallangot.—Preparations for sport.—Forest and jungle.—In the jaws of a tiger.—Extent of my injuries.—Kindness of a native woman.—Several tigers shot by my companions.—A native clawed.—Destruction of human life by wild beasts.—Trophies of the chase.—Resume our journey.—Difficulties of travelling in the forest. Rate of progress.—Deer shot.

On the 16th of October, at half-past six in the morning, we resumed our journey. The main road turns off, at Sittang, to Beeling; but a good native pathway runs eastward, the direction in which we wished to proceed. Close under the walls of Sittang there were some fields of rice and other grain, but within three or four miles of the city, and whilst its spires and domes were still visible in the distance, all signs that the land was under cultivation ceased. The last cultivated patch passed was a plantation of bananas, near which was a small hamlet, consisting of about half a dozen huts. Lofty trees skirted the path, and were scattered sparsely over the plain; but large quantities of timber had been felled in this neighbourhood at some time, and at present the ground was covered with a growth of jungle, young trees, and bamboo canes. The face of the country maintained this character for about eight miles, when we again met with extensive rice, maize, and wheat fields, and plantations of bananas, cotton, and indigo. The ground was level, and about two miles ahead, as we thought, we could see a large village; but we found it was at least double the distance off we had calculated.

Arriving at the village we found it very inconvenient to wait until the baggage came up, and we resolved that in future it should be sent on ahead instead of being left to follow in our rear. There were not many people in the village, the bulk of them being at work in the fields. Amongst those who came to look at us was a Buddhist priest, who spoke Hindostanee sufficiently well to make himself intelligible to Captain Lacy. He asked for money, and we gave him a couple of annas, and proceeded to make use of him by telling him to ask some of the people to find us a lodging. He said he could provide us, and led us to a dilapidated shed, for the use of which he was careful to inform us we would have to pay six annas a night. As we had no intention of occupying it for more than a few hours we did not haggle about the payment, though ten to one the hut was not this fellow's property. From him we learned that the name of the village was Patandah; that the inhabitants were mostly engaged in agriculture, and disposed of their produce at Sittang. The number of inhabitants in the village he stated to be ten thousand, an assertion that made us stare. From the number of huts and houses that we saw we concluded that two thousand would be nearer the mark.

The oxen came up a little before mid-day, looking fresh considering their twelve miles' march, and we pitched our tent outside the village. Just at this time a great many of the natives came in from their work, and speedily formed a large ring about us. They undoubtedly thought us great curiosities; and our horses also came in for a share of the public attention, being apparently considered as much of a novelty as wild beasts in England. These people, like all other Burmese, were vivacious and noisy, and it added materially to our comfort when they dispersed and went about their business. Our friend the Buddhist, however, established himself amongst us, palpably in the hopes of what the Scotch call "wee pickings." To get rid of him we offered him some devilled ham, taking care to explain what it was. He was off like a shot.

Having made inquiries, and found that no tigers or other large game were usually to be found within seven or eight miles of the neighbourhood, we went out in the evening with our fowling-pieces to shoot birds. In the space of two hours and a half our three guns had bagged fifty-three partridges, besides several birds of the snipe genus. Mr. Grant also shot a very beautiful pheasant. The partridges were found mostly about the maize-fields—the snipes near a small stream that ran round the northern side of the village.

Upon returning to our camping-place we were much amused by the extraordinary sagacity displayed by an elephant. These animals, I need scarcely mention, are universally used as beasts of burden throughout Southern

Asia. About a hundred yards from our tent two men had been engaged for some time in making and baking huge corn cakes for feeding the elephants. When these cakes were served out, each of the sagacious brutes carefully weighed them with its trunk, to ascertain that it had its due allowance. One elephant was dissatisfied, and sulkily threw its cake on one side, and refused to eat till the keeper had made good the deficiency. I recollect (the reader will pardon me for going out of my way to relate the anecdote) another singular incident that I witnessed in Bengal. Some troops were changing quarters, and an artillery field-forge was packed upon the back of an elephant. The poor brute was willing to carry it all with the exception of one of the heavy wheels, and as fast as this wheel was placed upon its back it threw it off. The keeper beat and stabbed the poor creature most unmercifully with an iron hook, similar in shape to a boat-hook; but in vain. The elephant left the cantonment without the obnoxious wheel.

Oct. 17.—Sent the servants forward about

six o'clock, with directions as to route, and orders to halt as soon as the oxen betrayed signs of fatigue. The interpreter, Angbang, we kept behind to accompany us, as it was our intention to ride slowly. After leaving Patandah, we soon entered a very wild and broken tract of country, with a bad native road running through its midst. Four miles from the village we came to a river, bridged with a very rickety wooden structure, so that we thought it necessary to use the precaution of dismounting, and crossing one at a time. Two villages and a few cultivated fields were passed in the next three or four miles, and the road then ran through a dense and gloomy forest, where the path was only just wide enough to permit us to ride in file. In another two hours we came up with the servants, who had pitched the tent, and lighted watch-fires. This was the first night we had camped away from the vicinity of human habitation.

The following morning we started with the baggage, and speedily came to a large river, fully a hundred yards wide. We soon discovered, however, that it was fordable. All these rivers and streams recently passed, may be tributaries to the Sittang or Salween. Nothing worthy of note occurred during the day. Passing through a fine, forest-covered country, but no signs seen of inhabitants. Just before halting crossed another stream of large size. Three miles farther came to a small hamlet. The people displayed the same inquisitiveness met with at all other places hitherto passed; but received us kindly enough.

Oct. 19.—By eight o'clock this morning we had arrived on the right bank of the great Salween River. It was, at the point where we struck it, quite half a mile wide, both banks being fringed with splendid forest trees. How to get transported to the opposite side was a difficulty that caused us a great deal of anxiety. Our best and wisest course appeared to be to proceed southwards along the bank until we came to some village where boats could be obtained.

We followed this plan, and soon came to

a small hamlet, abreast of which, on the opposite shore, was another and much larger village. The only boats procurable here were so small that the oxen had to be ferried over one at a time: consequently more than two hours were lost in conveying the whole of the baggage and servants across, and we decided to spend the night where we were. We could not learn the name of the smaller village: the one where we stayed was called Shallangat. It possessed several good houses, the residences of the native magistrates and chief men, and four temples.

The exact point at which we crossed the Salween, I cannot tell; but suppose it to be about eighty or ninety miles above Martaban. Several alligators were seen in the river, and troops of monkeys, and parrots in great variety, in the forests; but as yet we had not seen any large game. At Shallangat, however, we were informed that wild elephants and tigers, as well as deer and wild boars, were numerous in the adjoining forests; and we determined to have a day or two's sport before leaving this place.

We did not lodge in the village, but pitched our tent near the river, and the servants erected rude shanties of boughs and long grass for their own accommodation. The nights had been cold lately, and the heat, during daytime, never greater than 79°, and often as low as 68° and 70°.

Oct. 20.—We were up and ready for action by four o'clock, having engaged two of the village shekaries the preceding night. They put in an appearance punctually; but accompanied by fifty or sixty of the villagers to serve as beaters. As we felt quite competent to beat up our own game, and only required guiding to the spot where it was to be found, we gave these gentry to understand that if they went we should expect to have their services gratuitously, especially as we were doing them a favour in helping to rid the country of a great pest. The hint was sufficient. Finding they had nothing to expect in the way of reward, they declined to expose their precious persons, and fell away to their business two or three at a time.

Striking off almost due south, we followed a narrow footpath through a dense forest where daylight was nearly excluded, our native huntsmen leading the way. The trees were at least a hundred and fifty feet in height, and matted together with gigantic creepers bearing flowers of most gorgeous colours and patterns. After four miles or so, we made a direct turn to the left, and shortly afterward emerged from the forest on to a jungle-covered plain of considerable extent. Patches of bamboo thicket were here numerous, and afforded, our guide said, an usual lurking-place for tigers and boars. We accordingly made dispositions for the attack, ranging the shekaries and servants—of whom we had brought four with us besides Akbar, and Laoo (my own servant)—in a line with intervals, and placing ourselves near the centre. Advancing slowly, we beat every patch of long grass and clump of bushes that was large enough to conceal any animal of size. The first game started was a large boar, which made off at a great rate, and was speedily followed by two more of its disturbed companions. We did not interfere with them, our object being to shoot tigers, of which we began to fear there was not so many in the neighbourhood as our guide had represented. After three hours' fatiguing work we had reached the eastern extremity of the plain, and found ourselves amongst some low hillocks, fairly sprinkled over with large trees, and covered with tall, rank grass, where we made a halt for rest and refreshments. In the afternoon we continued our march, but with no signs of being likely to meet with sport, and about four o'clock we turned towards our camp. We marched along carelessly, without observing order or caution, and were not prepared to take advantage of Akbar's warning, when he exclaimed, "Beware, sahib," and a full-grown tiger went past us at a gallop. A straggling volley was fired after it, and though evidently not struck, the beast stopped, and rearing itself up on its hind-legs clawed the bark of a tree, just as a cat scratches the leg of a chair or table. Mr. Grant and myself fired simultaneously, but without effect, and before a thought of the creature's intention had time to flash through my mind, I was down under its paws.

Seizing me by the left thigh, the tiger shook me as a dog shakes a rat; and then, growling horribly, dragged me at a tremendous rate through the thick undergrowth of the forest. I heard the frightened shouts of my companions and the report of several shots, and then a dizziness came over me; but I did not lose consciousness. As I was jolted through the forest I several times caught hold of the trees, but the tiger, growling fiercely, shook me free in an' instant. All this time, though quite calm and collected, I felt a strong desire to preserve my existence, and never for a moment experienced that apathy with regard to my danger that some persons have described under similar circumstances.

How long I was in the jaws of this brute I cannot tell. It seemed to me an age before the creature stopped. My companions afterwards declared that I had been dragged at least half a mile from the spot where I was first seized. They followed as fast as they could run, and though I was unaware of it at the time, never lost sight of the beast. To this circumstance I undoubtedly owe my life: for had there been any delay in rendering me assistance it must have been fatal to me.

The moment the tiger halted it released my thigh, and seemed to be attracted by the approach of my companions; though, as yet, I did not see them myself. Taking advantage of this release, I tried to creep to the shelter of some tall bushes near at hand. In an instant, and with a terrible roar, the creature pounced upon me, seizing me this time by the shoulder, and at the same time lacerating my chest with its claws. A shot was fired, and I heard the bullet whistle overhead. Fear of hitting me had caused them to fire too high. A second and third shot were equally unsuccessful; and the tiger, again releasing me, began to lick up the blood which oozed through my jacket. I began to feel very faint, and could not suppress a groan. Several times the tiger dabbed his paws, apparently in play, about my face, but did not use its claws, fortunately for me. Presently the beast seemed to be seized with a sudden rage, and commenced to spit like an angry cat at some one approaching, whose footsteps I could hear, but I could not see him owing to my position, for I was lying flat on my back. There was the sharp bang of a rifle close to my head, a heavy weight fell across me, and then I comprehended that my brave friend, Grant, was pulling me from under the dead body of the tiger.

Captain Lacy and some of the others came up, and proceeded to staunch the flow of blood from my wounds. That on my thigh was the worst injury. The flesh was bitten and torn to such an extent that the bone was visible. The wounds on the chest were also severe; but my shoulder was not much injured. When the bleeding was stopped I fainted, and upon recovering consciousness, found I was being carried along upon a rough litter formed of boughs. I suffered great pain, especially in the leg: and was exceedingly thankful when we arrived at our camping place.

As soon as the news spread about Shallangat that a tiger had been slain, the people came crowding round our tent to see it. The hubbub they created was horrible. There was shouting, singing, beating of tomtoms and drums, blowing of reeds, dancing and exulting over the dead animal. In my weak state the noise was particularly irritating; and as it was in vain to appeal to the sympathies of these people, the dead beast was removed to a distance, where the rejoicing continued nearly all night.

The following day fever had set in, and towards mid-day I became delirious. With a few lucid intervals, I was in this state for five days.

Oct. 26.—Better to-day, but very weak and unable to move. In the evening the wound in my thigh commenced bleeding afresh.

Great trouble in staunching it, and I lost consciousness for two hours.

OCT. 28.—Very weak and low spirited. My companions manifest much uneasiness about my wound. It looks as though about to mortify. Next day: better, but signs of inflammation.

OCT. 30.—A very hot day. Thermometer 92° in the shade. Suffered excruciating pain, and became thoroughly exhausted.

Nov. 3.—Cannot tell whether I shall recover or not. Pain almost unendurable, and wound looks very bad. A native woman brought me a dish of boiled rice and chopped gourds. The poor creature was evidently anxious to do what she could, and we sent her away with a reward for her kindness. I need scarcely say that I had no stomach for her mess.

Nov. 8.—Seem to be on the road to recovery. Wound healing nicely, and I can read and write.

Nov. 15.—Managed to walk a few paces to-day. Return of health and strength only a matter of time now. Since my illness, have been most kindly and attentively nursed by Captain Lacy, Mr. Grant, my servant Laoo, and others of our attendants. Lacy and Grant have been out shooting several times, and met with good sport. On the 12th, three tigers were killed; on the 13th, one; and on the following day an inhabitant of Shallangat fell in the way of an enraged and wounded tiger, and was badly clawed before he could be rescued. Captain Lacy says that the tigers of this neighbourhood are the fiercest he has met with, and the natives assure us that frequently two or three persons are carried of and killed by wild beasts in the space of a month. They manifest the greatest joy and excitement when a tiger is killed. Their only means of destroying them is by poison and pitfalls, as they are far too timid to face the beast when at large.

Amongst other trophies of the chase secured by my companions, were a wild boar or two, a very handsome leopard, and several antelopes or deer, besides an innumerable number of birds, and other small game.

Nov. 20.—As I felt well and strong enough to ride to-day, we left Shallangat in the afternoon, and passing very near the scene of my accident, continued our journey through the forest eastward. On my account the distance traversed did not exceed eight miles, and the tent was pitched in the depth of one of the most noble and magnificent forests I have ever seen. The trees were of great height, with splendid foliage and coloured blossom, and swarmed with gorgeous parrots and other birds. There was no path, and in many places the servants were obliged to cut away the thicket and creepers before the horses and oxen could effect a passage. Travelling was thus rendered troublesome, and we had to keep a sharp look-out lest the creepers which ran across our road should become entwined around the horses' legs. Near our camping place was a stream of beautifully clear water, about five feet deep, but having pools of ten or twelve feet in depth. Immense shoals of small fish were seen in it, though all our efforts to catch some of them were unavailing.

Nov. 21.—Left our ground about seven o'clock. The oxen and horses swam across the stream, the men wading over with the baggage. Our progress was very slow indeed, owing to the closeness of the undergrowth and the strength of the creepers, which sometimes nearly dragged us off our horses as we rode against them. The forest appears to be becoming more dense, and many monkeys as well as parrots harbour in the tree-tops.

After being on the move six hours, we calculated we had not advanced more than twelve miles. Next day we were quite as much retarded, and suffered some inconvenience from want of water. The distance got over was not above ten miles. On the 23rd, however, there was a change in the character of the country; and though it was still almost entirely covered with forest, it was not so close, and was less choked up with undergrowth. Water was also abundant, several brooks and rivulets being passed. The distance marched this day would be about fifteen miles, partly in a north-east and partly in an east direction.

In the evening we went on foot in search of game. Near one of the brooks we found the fresh footmarks of deer; and, after tracing them for four or five miles, came up with a large herd of antelopes, of which we shot three. A fourth was wounded, but as we might have had to follow it for miles, we did not pursue it. On our way back to camp we amused ourselves with pheasant-shooting, the birds being numerous and of most magnificent plumage.

CHAPTER III.

Party of natives and their village.—Paucity of large game met with.—Rough ground.—Wild elephants.—One of them shot.—Elephants' feet not a dainty.—The river Thungyen. — Cobras and green snakes. — Our servants lost.—A night out and its drawbacks.—Wild beasts and their fondness for water.—Captain Lacy goes in search of the men.—The luggage arrives.—The passage of the river.—A day's rest.—Results of an evening's shooting.—Impenetrable forests compel us to make detours.—Change in the character of the country.—Plains covered with beautiful flowers.—Average distance an ox can travel.—Arrive at a large village.—Surrounded by the crowd.—A native girl seized by a tiger.—Number of natives killed by tigers.

Nov. 24.—During the last few days we have seen no signs of the inhabitants of the country, but this morning, soon after starting, we came upon nine natives cutting wood, and they pointed out to us the road to their village. We found a good beaten track, and in less than half an hour reached the hamlet, which was surrounded by about a score acres of rice and maize fields. We passed through it without stopping, exciting a great deal of attention from the natives; not unmixed, apparently, with astonishment and curiosity as to our business there.

The country eastward of the village was flat in the extreme, but the scenery pretty, and streams of water numerous, though all of them were mere rivulets in size. The trees consisted principally of palms, oak, ebony, banyans, and a great variety of beautiful, feathery - foliaged bamboos. The taller trees forming the forests were of species unknown to any of our party. Some delicious peaches were found growing wild; but although this tract of country was very thinly inhabited— almost deserted in fact—we saw no signs of wild animals: indeed, hitherto no game has been seen except when special search has been made for it; yet, according to native accounts, the neighbourhood swarms with tigers, leopards, and antelopes. Birds and monkeys are very plentiful.

As one of our chief objects in undertaking this journey was to enjoy sport on fresh ground, we determined, after a long consultation, to halt at the next convenient spot, and thoroughly explore the country through which we were passing. A spot, however, to suit our taste was not found this day, and the next, leaving the servants to push forward alone, with orders to halt about mid-day if they did not meet with a village, we rode off in search of a little excitement, taking with us our interpreter, Angbang, who professed to have some knowledge of this region, and another man to look after the horses, should we have occasion to leave them behind at any point.

The ground was rough in places and trying for the horses, and we were delayed some time by Mr. Grant's horse casting a shoe, which had to be replaced before we could proceed. Northward an extensive forest seemed to threaten an impediment to our progress in that direction, and we therefore rode in a north-east course, the two men keeping up with our horses without trouble, notwithstanding the irregularity of the ground, which soon became undulating and hilly. Between ten and eleven o'clock we came within sight of a river, the course of which was traceable for several miles. To this river we began to make our way, and when within half a mile of its bank, discovered a herd of about sixty elephants quietly browsing on the plain. We had not expected to meet with such large game as this; but quickly dismounting, we left the horses in charge of the men, and advanced on foot. There were plenty of trees scattered about, and forming groves here and there, so that we were able to get close to the elephants without being observed by the wary animals. We decided that all three of us should fire at the same beast, myself and Mr. Grant aiming behind the ear, and Captain Lacy at the shoulder. It was some time before we could get a favourable opportunity for firing; for the elephants kept very close together, and the largest animal which we wished to kill was surrounded by its companions. In trying to creep round to a better position we were discovered, and the herd commenced to move away, though not very quickly, the large male coming to the rear as if to cover their retreat. He stood looking at us, his great ears twitching nervously, and his trunk rolled up in a coil. Myself and Grant were for firing at once; but Captain Lacy declared that to aim at the front would be useless: while he and Grant, therefore, moved cautiously round to the creature's left flank, I kept in front to attract its attention and prevent it from turning to face them. The report of their rifles rang out sharply, and reverberated across the plain, and for a moment the elephant stood as if stunned, and then ran quickly to a small tree, against which it leaned so heavily that the trunk snapped in two, and the poor beast fell with a shock that shook the ground perceptibly. As it was making violent efforts to rise again I fired at it, and my companions gave it the contents of their second barrels. While we were reloading, our victim lashed the ground angrily, and with its proboscis made the gravel fly for many yards around. To ease it of pain as quickly as possible, we went quite close to deliver our second volley, upon which it extended its trunk towards us and trumpeted defiantly. Three more shots, and the gigantic frame stiffened rigidly. To my mind there was something sad, yet sublime, in the death of the huge beast, and I was almost sorry to think I had had a hand in the slaughter of it.

We secured the tusks, the feet, and a little of the flesh, and leaving the immense carcass to decay where it had fallen, rode away. The excitement had been too great to admit of our noticing the movements of the remainder of the herd, and they were quite out of sight now.

We had eaten nothing since early morning, and were, in consequence, very hungry. Riding down to the river, therefore, we watered our horses, and made preparations for a meal. The elephant's feet and flesh were roasted, we being anxious to follow the example of other travellers, and taste the novelty. The novelty, however, was all about it worthy of praise; and we would have much preferred a little venison, or better still, good English beef.

After carefully consulting a map and considering our past route, we felt certain that the river upon whose bank we were resting must be the Thungyen, in which case we were within seventy or eighty miles of the town or city of Lahaing, where it was our intention to make a call. The bend of the river at this point was about five hundred yards wide, the stream running due north with a rather rapid current. The banks were prettily clothed with trees and jungle, the creepers and parasitical plants hanging down from the branches of the former into the water like lines. A great many snakes harboured in the long grass near the water, amongst which we recognized several of the deadly cobras or hooded snakes, and a pretty little green, mottled reptile, about fifteen inches in length, which I believe is common all over India.

We knew that our servants would be sure to halt when they came to this river, and we therefore moved southwards, expecting to find them encamped on its bank. To our surprise and annoyance, however, we rode eight or nine miles without meeting with them, and came to the conclusion that they had halted before reaching the river. Both ourselves and horses were very tired, as well as the two men, and it was evident we could not ride much farther; but the nights being generally chilly, it was not pleasant to look forward to a bivouac on the ground without the shelter of tent and blanket, and as we had come farther south than the men could possibly have done, we rode some distance back again, still in the hope that they would come up. Nothing was seen of them, and no answering shots greeting those that were fired to attract attention, we picketed the horses in the most sheltered nook we could find, and lay on the ground in our cloaks near them. Notwithstanding the heat of a large fire we suffered much from cold and damp, and were continually disturbed by the wild beasts which came to the river for the purpose of drinking and bathing. It was sufficiently star-light for us to see herds of elephants, rhinoceroses, antelopes, deer and buffaloes; and we heard the roar of tigers and other beasts of prey. Considering how comparatively little large game we had hitherto met with, a surprising number of wild animals visited the water during the night.

It is needless to say we were on the

move as soon as it was daylight. Going down to the river to perform our ablutions, we met a small herd of antelopes, and shot a couple of them. About five o'clock we sent off the two men in search of Akbar and the baggage; and Captain Lacy rode away on the same errand, all three of them going in different directions. Hour after hour passed, and neither the messengers nor the others appeared, and the anxiety of myself and Mr. Grant began to give place to a feeling of absolute alarm. At length, between eight and nine o'clock, the baggage train was seen slowly making its way down to the river, a full mile farther down the stream. In answer to our shouts* the men altered their course, and made direct for the spot where we stood. They had seen nothing of Captain Lacy or either of the two men, and said they had passed the night about an hour and a half's march from the river, not being aware of its proximity until this morning. An hour

* In the calm still plains of a wild country, the shout of a man can be heard distinctly for from a mile and a half to two or even three miles, according to position, &c.

later, Angbang and the other man came in. They had, after a long search, found the track of the oxen, and followed it until they rejoined us, being unable to overtake them before. It was vexatious that Captain Lacy did not know this, as he was evidently putting himself to the trouble of a tiring and useless search.

A new difficulty was now before us—the passage of the river. After discussing many different means of crossing it, we decided to swim the cattle over, and construct a raft for the conveyance of the goods. We all set to work immediately, and soon had a tolerably large, though somewhat rough, raft. We found upon trial that it would float all our goods safely; and we proceeded to make some rude paddles for its guidance and propulsion.

About noon, Captain Lacy came back, very much vexed at the unnecessary trouble to which he had been subjected, and with his horse nearly knocked up. After dinner and a short rest, we embarked, three of the men swimming over to guide the cattle and horses, the remainder of us taking post on the raft. Captain Lacy had a smaller raft put together for the conveyance of his own horse, as it did not appear equal to the exertion of so long a swim. The oxen and horses got across in about half an hour, but the rafts were not so successful. They proved unmanageable, and drifted five miles or more down the stream. Lacy's horse became frightened and restive, got off the raft into the water, dragging its master with it, and narrowly escaped drowning. When at length we reached the opposite shore, we were all so tired as to be scarcely able to pitch the tent, and make the necessary arrangements for passing the night comfortably. We were too exhausted to be much disturbed by the howls of wild beasts; but we took the necessary precaution of lighting fires all round our encampment as a protection to the oxen and horses.

Nov. 27.—All the party, and the horses, showing traces of fatigue, we determined to remain in camp to-day for a thorough rest.

In the evening, myself, Grant, and Lacy shot over the ground in the neighbourhood of our tent. The result was a small antelope, thirty common Indian partridges, five superb pheasants, and a few parrots. A very small and lively kind of monkey is here numerous, but they keep in the tops of the tallest trees, far out of reach of small-shot. Two cobras were seen and killed. The largest was six feet in length. These horrid creatures seem too plentiful to be pleasant, considering their bite is usually fatal in the space of two or three hours. A few other snakes were seen, but of a harmless species, and a great variety of lizards.

Nov. 28.—Immediately after breakfast we resumed our journey, keeping as nearly due east as the nature of the country would permit. Much forest lay in our way; some patches of it so dense that we were compelled to make long detours to round it, in consequence of which the actual distance advanced towards the city of Lahaing, where we intended to make a halt, was not more than six miles, though we had probably marched more than double that distance.

Many gutta-percha trees were seen to-day, some of them eighty or ninety feet in height, and seven or eight in diameter. A large portion of the forest was composed of teak trees of large dimensions; there were also other trees of species unknown to us, though I fancy we recognized the lime.

Nov. 29.—Marked change in the character of the country. Still considerable tracts of forest, but some fine open plains sprinkled with clumps of trees. After advancing eight miles we found the ground hilly, but speaking at a rough guess, none of the elevations were more than two hundred feet above the neighbouring country. About one o'clock a small herd of antelope passed in front of us. We could not get near them, and after several harmless shots they got clear away.

I have never seen more beautiful flowers than those that grew upon these plains and hills. They appeared principally to be a kind of lily, of various colours, red, yellow, white, and some variegated, and growing to the height of our horses' girths. There was also a very pretty blue flower with a charming scent, and growing so thickly that the ground seemed from a distance to be of a bright blue colour, with here and there patches of red, yellow, and white, where the lilies predominated. We passed the night upon one of these plains.

Nov. 30.—The country being favourable—that is tolerably open, with good grassy plains—we performed a long march, advancing quite sixteen miles. I speak of this as a long march because we had found by experience that the oxen were not capable of travelling more than eight or ten miles a day on an average. Towards the close of this day's journey the country once more assumed a thickly wooded appearance; but we saw no animal life, with the exception of birds. At three o'clock in the afternoon we came within sight of a large village, and an hour later arrived at it. Our arrival, as was invariably the case at all villages we came to, caused a great commotion amongst the natives, and apparently some little fear, as the women and children screamed outrageously; but when we commenced to quietly erect our tent on a convenient grassy space near the centre of the village, a crowd of the inhabitants gathered round us, squatting on their haunches, and watching us attentively; and they remained until we had cooked our dinner and commenced to eat it. As the close proximity of four or five hundred people (there was fully that number) was not pleasant, we instructed Angbang, our interpreter, to request them to disperse. They did so instantly and quickly, and only a few of the men remained watching us from a respectful distance. In the evening we walked about the village and tried to make ourselves friendly with the people. We were only partially successful, as they seemed to have a sort of dread or awe of us. One old man whom we attracted to us and questioned through Angbang, informed us that very few of the villagers had seen a European before, and it was more than thirty years since a white man had passed through the village. Who this white man was, or what was his business there, we could not ascertain; but our informant declared that he was accompanied by a large party of natives from the north (*i.e.* Burmen, or perhaps Hindoos, I cannot be sure which was meant), who travelled on horseback, and had pack horses with them. We could not imagine who this traveller could have been, or form any probable conjectures upon the subject.

During the night we were disturbed by a frightful outcry amongst the natives, which lasted some time, and was followed by an incessant drumming until daylight. As all the natives of India, Burmah, and Siam are exceedingly noisy and fond of beating drums, tomtoms, &c., we did not take much notice of the disturbance except to anathematize the authors of it. In the morning, however, the same old man with whom we had spoken on the previous evening, came to our tent, and informed us that a young girl had been carried away by a tiger. The tiger had entered the hut where she was sleeping, and having first apparently killed her with a blow from its paw, carried off the body. The whole affair was witnessed by seven or eight female occupants of the hut, and by several other persons who were moving about the village street at the time, for it occurred soon after midnight—a time when most natives are still moving about—but no attempt had been made to follow the beast or compel it to relinquish its prey. "What is to be will be," is a favourite maxim with these people, or rather, indeed, a rule of life; and to such an extent do they carry their apathetic submission to fate, that they will not even use remedies in cases of disease or bites of numerous reptiles—at least if the said remedies are European—although they may have witnessed their successful application by foreigners.

This, it seems, was not the first visit the

tiger had paid to the village, and during the last four months no less than nineteen persons had been slain by wild beasts, the majority of them, our old friend asserted, by this particular tiger. Of these nineteen, eleven were children, and one a native hunter, who had lost his life in endeavouring to destroy the fearful man-eater. Besides the poor girl who was killed last night, four children and one adult had actually been fetched out of the huts by this audacious beast, yet the men of the village had not sufficient pluck to attempt its destruction.

We were further informed that a year or two ago, the tigers were so numerous and destructive to human life that the inhabitants of a village about half a day's journey to the southward, had been compelled to abandon their houses and take up their residences in this place, which, by-the-by, is called Sattybardah. The man-eating tiger was supposed to have his lair somewhere in the neighbourhood of this deserted village. We soon determined to know where its lair was, and while we cleaned our rifles and made other preparations, Angbang was sent with the old man to try and persuade some of the villagers to go with us as guides. A couple of score of volunteers presented themselves for this service, and we selected six of the most likely-looking fellows in addition to the old man himself. We also took with us Laoo, and two others of our servants, who were all armed with muskets.

CHAPTER IV.

Traces of the accident.—Preparations for the destruction of the tiger.—Remains of the victim.—Unsuccessful search.—A deserted village—A leopard shot.—Captain Lacy's account of his adventure with a tiger.—A native badly hurt.—Return to Sattybardah.—Offer a reward for the discovery of the man-eater's lair.—Evidences of its dreadfully destructive powers.—Prepare to meet our antagonist.—A double adventure.—Marvellous tenacity of life.—Excitement at Sattybardah on the news of our success.—Size and weight of the tigers.—Large bag of game made on the 4th of December.—Indian bird of paradise.—Bees.—Parrots.—Villages.—Tormented by mosquitoes.

PREVIOUSLY to starting in search of our game we went to view the spot where the girl was seized. It was a large oblong hut with a doorway at one end. The only traces of the catastrophe to be seen were a few large spots of blood, and some marks of the tiger's claws on the hard earth of the floor, as though the beast had made several long scratches. There were, also, four distinct marks of its claws on the wood-work of the threshold, as well as blood smeared about; the doorway being so narrow that the creature seemed to have had some difficulty in forcing itself and its dead or unconscious burden through the confined opening. Outside, other blood spots were visible upon the ground, traceable, according to reports, for about half a mile; but no one had had courage to follow this dreadful clue to the course of the beast further. So great was the consternation, that not a single man had gone to his work in the fields, and the people seemed almost afraid to appear in the streets of the village.

When we started on our errand of revenge, a large crowd of men and women escorted us to the outskirts of the village, singing, shouting, and beating small drums, blowing cow-horns, and pipes, and creating altogether a most horrible hubbub, intended to encourage us and strengthen our nerves for the forthcoming fight with the bloodthirsty monarch of the forest. Our nerves, however, needed little bracing, for we were all three itching to meet this monster and put it beyond the power of doing further mischief.

We traced the blood spots for two miles, and at places where the body had been forced through the bushes, found fragments of the girl's clothing hanging on the thorns. There were also many marks of the tiger's feet, so that we had no difficulty in following the track. About two miles and a half from Sattybardah, we came to the spot where the beast had made his feast. The victim's bones were strewn about, some of them not thoroughly stripped of the flesh. The left thigh and the pelvis remained untouched; and the head was also found, but with the face horribly gnawed and disfigured. The ground was covered with blood and fragments of the poor creature's clothing. After collecting together in a sack all the remains that could be found, and sending a man back to the village with them, we commenced to beat all the thickets and brakes within a mile around, but without finding the tiger. This was rather strange, as these animals after eating a meal always retire a short distance and sleep for some hours. Our guides insisted that the lair of the beast we were in search of was near the village mentioned above, and said we should find it there; but we were of a different opinion, as it was out of all reason to suppose a fed tiger would go a distance described as half a day's journey. However, a long search convinced us that there was no chance of meeting with our man-eater here, and we determined to proceed to the village in question, in the hope of meeting with sport of some sort. An old native pathway pointed out the direction we were to take, and a wilder forest track I have seldom passed through. Not only were the trees exceedingly lofty and thickly matted with parasitical plants; but the ground was much intersected with rocky ravines, at the bottom of most of which small streams of water ran. Three small herds of antelopes were met with, and five of the animals were killed, each weighing about forty or fifty pounds. We had marched a good twelve miles before the village was reached, and so much time had been consumed, that it was then drawing towards evening.

The village was a most desolate and dreary-looking place; the houses in ruins, many of them with the roofs rotting away, some already fallen in. The fields in its neighbourhood, once well cultivated, were become a wilderness, overgrown with shrubs and jungle plants. The stillness of death reigned about the place, but as we walked amongst the huts, many small beasts of prey rushed out through the half-blocked doorways and holes in the walls. They appeared principally to be a species of hyæna, and some wild cats of large size. One leopard tried to escape from a dilapidated hut near the centre of the village, but speedily rolled in the dust, pierced by five bullets.

The best conditioned hut having been selected for our temporary habitation, fires were lighted and we proceeded to cook a meal of antelope venison. When this repast was over it was about seven o'clock, a time when the beasts of prey are moving about in search of a quarry, and we sallied forth to make another search for our man-eating tiger, though with small hopes of meeting with it so far away from the scene of its bloody exploit. We divided our attendants into two parties, Captain Lacy proceeding with one division to the right of the village, myself and Mr. Grant leading the other in a westerly direction. We thoroughly searched the country for about three miles, but saw no game save a few hyænas, some monkeys and birds. About nine o'clock, however, we heard shots fired in quick succession in the distance, and knowing that the sounds must proceed from Captain Lacy's party, we hastened back as quickly as possible. Other shots followed, and when, about three quarters of an hour afterwards, we arrived at the village, we found Captain Lacy there with the body of a tiger which he had shot close at hand. It was six feet six inches in length from the nose to the tail; but the natives said it was much smaller than the man-eater which we were in search of; and we also were pretty confident that we should not meet with the terror of Sattybardah so far away from that village.

Captain Lacy's tiger, however, had afforded some sport and not bitten the dust without showing its claws. The following is Captain Lacy's own account of his adventure.

"There was not sufficient moon to give any light, but the stars were shining brightly, and a sort of twilight still prevailed, so that objects were distinctly visible. I could see the monkeys moving noiselessly about in the tree-tops as our passage disturbed them, and looking like weird spectres in the gloom of night. I was walking a little in advance of the others, the natives being evidently rather fearful of exposing themselves to any sudden attack. While I was diligently beating the bushes in front, it seems the natives had an eye to the possibility of an attack from behind, and it was well for them that they had, for my servant, Angbang, all at once called my attention to a movement of the long grass in our rear, as though some animal was following us. I halted, and the servants slinked behind me, placing me between themselves and the suspicious movement, or, I should say, the place where it had been observed; for the instant we came to a standstill, the waving of the grass ceased. I tried to persuade the blacks to beat up the quarters of our foe which, I felt sure was a tiger; but the cowardly rascals only shrunk farther off, and even my own two men refused to obey orders. So in at it I went alone. With a savage, barking sort of growl, the tiger flew out at me, and made a tremendous spring before I had time to fire. By stooping I avoided the beast, which went over my head and alighted six or seven feet beyond me. He had the contents of my two barrels in his body in a twinkling, and either in agony or rage, rolled over and over like a child at play; then got up and galloped straight at the blacks, who fled like a flock of sheep. But pussy got hold of one fellow in spite of the shots fired by his companions, and I think I never in my life heard a man howl so pitifully. Approaching close enough to make certain of my aim, I gave pussy two more bullets from my spare rifles, and she died with scarcely any contractions of the muscles, such as are observable in all animals, more or less, when mortally wounded."

The man who had fallen into the clutches of this tiger was badly hurt. The creature had struck him a blow upon the shoulder with its paw, tearing the flesh from the bone, and leaving it hanging in strips. The wound presented a shocking spectacle, and the poor fellow undoubtedly suffered great pain. We stitched it up, and bandaged the arm as well as we could under the circumstances; and administered a little brandy to the man. He is one of the men from Sattybardah.

Dec. 2.—We decided this morning to return to Sattybardah; and following the same road we had come by, we arrived there about mid-day. There was great enthusiasm in the village when the skin of the tiger was displayed, somewhat damped, however, at sight of the injured man, and the knowledge that our trophy had not belonged to the terrible man-eater.

Dec. 3.—We caused it to be made known throughout the village, that we would make another effort to find and destroy the tiger which had proved such a terrible pest to its inhabitants; and offered a reward to any one who could discover and lead us to the haunt of the beast, but few seemed to care to be engaged in such a search, however tempting the guerdon. We sent out our own servants and such of the villagers as offered themselves; they returned very much alarmed, declaring they had seen the tiger close to the spot where the remains of the native girl were found the day before yesterday. In ten minutes after the receipt of this news, we were on our way to the place, accompanied by nine or ten natives and servants.

Arriving on the ground, we spent three hours in a provokingly unsuccessful search for the wary monster. At the end of this time we had examined more ground than previously, and arrived near a deep and very steep-sided ravine. It struck both Captain Lacy and Mr. Grant that this ravine was just the sort of place a tiger would be likely to choose for its lair; and the natives thought so too, for they evinced great reluctance to descend into it. Cautiously making our way down—for the foothold was precarious owing to the looseness of the soil and steepness of the sides—we commenced a diligent search amongst the jungle at the bottom of the ravine. Footmarks of the tiger were abundant, many of them quite fresh; and, besides bones and other remains of an enormous number of antelopes and animals of the deer tribe, we found two human skulls, and some of the bones of five human bodies; but nothing was seen of the tiger itself. In many places the grass was crushed down, as if the animal had been sleeping upon the spot, and the bark of several small trees bore marks of the creature's claws.

We were quite sure that the tiger would return to this ravine, if it were not now lurking somewhere at hand; but as the presence of a large party of men so near its home might delay or prevent its approach, we dismissed all our attendants, who were nothing loath to depart, and prepared ourselves for the forthcoming contest. There were a number of loose blocks of stone lying about, and with some of these we built up a sort of parapet to serve as a rest for our rifles; then we sat down and quietly waited the return of the man-eater to its lair, scarcely venturing to talk to each other, lest the sound of our voices should alarm the brute.

Perhaps an hour had elapsed when a low purring growl warned us to be on the alert. The sound came from above, and looking up we perceived two large tigers on the edge of the ravine preparing to make a descent. They were favourably situated for a shot. Mr. Grant was the first to fire, and one brute fell to the bottom of the ravine, where it lay on its back feebly pawing the air. The second tiger elevated its hair like an angry cat, and growled fiercely at us, till the advent of two or three bullets put a stop to its noise, and it disappeared, being, apparently, badly hit.

We ran out of our shelter, and seeing

that the first tiger was lying motionless and evidently dead, ascended the side of the ravine as speedily as possible and pursued the wounded beast, which seemed to be anxious to make good its escape. The broad splashes of blood lay in its track so thickly that we were able to follow it at a run, and at the distance of half-a-mile or so, came up with it sprawling on the ground. It growled out a fierce defiance, but was too far gone to show fight: indeed, it scarcely needed a coup-de-grace. Afterwards, upon opening this tiger, we found it had been shot *through the heart;* and had actually ran full half-a-mile after receiving the mortal injury—one of the most remarkable incidents of the tenacity of animal life that ever came under my notice.

Returning to the ravine to make sure the other brute was quite hors de combat, we found that the single bullet fired by Mr. Grant had killed it; having entered the chest and travelled downwards into the body.

Leaving the tigers where they had fallen,

we returned to Sattybardah at once; and when our success was made known the excitement of the people was intense. They shouted and danced, and displayed the wildest gratitude towards us for ridding them of these fearful pests. A large crowd of the men rushed away to fetch the tigers, and when they returned all sorts of insults were heaped upon the now harmless foe. The dead brutes were mocked and reviled, beaten with sticks, kicked, spit upon, and dragged about until the skins were quite spoiled. The crowd also renewed the demonstration of their thankfulness towards us with so much enthusiasm, that we were glad to beat a retreat to our tent; whither, however, we were followed by the unpleasantly grateful villagers, who would not retire until repeatedly requested to do so. Throughout the night the rejoicings were kept up with so much hubbub and drumming, that we found repose impossible.

There could be no doubt but that one of the tigers we had slain was the beast who had killed so many of the villagers—indeed it is reasonable to suppose that they were both man-eaters. They were male and female. The female was much the largest, her length being seven feet eight inches exclusive of the tail, and she must have weighed at least six hundred pounds. The male was seven feet one inch in length, and he was altogether made more lightly than the female. His weight was probably no more than four hun. dred, or four hundred and fifty pounds; but we had no means of ascertaining exactly.

The 4th of December was spent in shooting birds and monkeys, and the following bag was made by our three guns : viz., seventeen monkeys, thirty-two parrots of four different species, ninety-five partridges; three birds of the heron or stork family, and eight birds known as the Indian bird of paradise. The monkeys were small, and of an ordinary kind, common all over Farther India. They, together with the parrots, were eagerly eaten by the natives to whom we gave them. The Indian partridges seem to me to be a connecting link between the partridge known to

Europeans and the quail. They are larger than the partridge found in England. The Indian bird of paradise is said by the natives of Bengal, where it is plentiful, to be the true bird of paradise. It is not much larger than a blackbird, and the plumage is black and yellow, with some brown about the tail. In shape it is similar to the New Guinea bird of paradise. They are hard to kill, and will carry more shot than a pigeon or rook. Wild bees are very plentiful in the forests around Sattybardah, and the decayed trees are full of their nests containing delicious honey. It is collected in large quantities by the women and boys of the village, who smoke the bees out, but sometimes get terribly stung. A lad was brought to us this evening with his face shockingly swollen, he having been attacked by the enraged insects. We did what we could for him, and saw him again the following morning when he was in a high state of fever.

DEC. 5.—We left Sattybardah about half-past ten, the heat being very moderate, and a pleasant breeze blowing from the west. The natives bade me adieu with shouts and much expression of goodwill. We have quite won the hearts of these people by our services in the tiger-shooting line. We did not find a regular beaten road far beyond the village, but the nature of the ground was such that travelling was not at all unpleasant or trying. The trees were here not so tall as those seen farther westward, but many of them were quite a hundred feet in height, and generally free from creepers and parasites. Neither were many monkeys seen in these trees; but parrots were abundant enough. We shot a few of a very pretty kind. The plumage was crimson, prettily variegated with black and ultramarine. The parrot most common in these parts is a green one with red markings, and we have seen it fluttering amongst the trees more or less since we left Rangoon. It is the size of the grey parrot or rather larger, and is commonly to be met with in the shops of European bird-fanciers.

Five or six miles from Sattybardah we

passed a small village on our right hand, and four miles farther another, also on the right, and distant about three miles. Both these villages were very small, and lay too much out of our course to be called at. There was a considerable space of cultivated land in their neighbourhood, five or six hundred acres, perhaps, consisting of rice and maize; and we thought it likely that this grain was grown for trading purposes at Lahaing, or some other large city. The ground was fertile and well watered; one stream that we found might almost be dignified with the title of a river. It was sixty or seventy yards broad, but fordable in places. Near this river was a maize-field, surrounded with a hedge of some thorny plant. It was kept closely cut, and from a distance looked like an English hedgerow. Many natives, both men and women, were at work in the fields; and a few of them left their employment to come and stare at us with eyes full of astonishment.

Our cattle having had a long and thorough rest at Sattybardah, we were enabled to push on nearly twenty miles before they showed signs of fatigue. Our first camping place was on the banks of a small stream; but this place swarmed with musquitoes, which tormented us and our cattle to such an extent that the latter became almost frantic, and tried hard to break from their picket-lines. We were in consequence compelled to move away from the water, and even then did not succeed in wholly escaping the annoyance of these pertinacious little wretches. My companions suffered less than myself, for they took refuge in clouds of tobacco smoke; but I am not a smoker, and, as Lacy facetiously remarked, my face soon looked like that of a prize-fighter after a pitched battle; and at length I was glad to purchase a reprieve from the torments at any cost, and overcoming my dislike of tobacco, placed a pipe between my lips.

CHAPTER V.

Our position.—Monotonous rustling of the leaves.—Signs of inhabitants. — Flat country. — Rhinoceroses. — Fruit.—Pagodas and Priests.—Civil disposition of the natives.—Siamese cities.—Lahaing.—Large number of tame elephants seen in the streets.—The city nuisances.—Anecdotes of hawks. — Cock-fighting. — Curious soap-stone ornaments.—Strange tricks of a travelling conjuror.—Pleasure evinced by the crowd.—Annoying insects and lizards, and nightmare.

December 6th.—We broke up our camp at six o'clock, and started with the intention of making a short day's journey of it, so as not to overtask the oxen. There is a great deal of forest about this country, which is undoubtedly very thinly inhabited, although we must be approaching the great city of Lahaing. We calculate we are about midway between the Thungyen and Menam rivers, and perhaps a little nearer to the latter.

It would be very hot to-day were it not for a strong breeze blowing from the south-west. This wind causes a singular monotonous rustling among the trees of the forest, sounding like the breaking of a heavy surf on the seashore. This region is solitary and desolate to a melancholy degree, and although there are traces that the plains are visited by herds of elephants and other large game, none are to be seen.

After advancing ten miles, we came to the outskirts of an extensive forest, and erected our tent. It was now only half-past ten o'clock in the morning, and we determined that towards evening (it is seldom that much game is to be met with except during early morning and evening) we would see what sport was to be had in this neighbourhood. Meantime, while wandering about in search of a shot at a bird or monkey, we came to a spot where several trees had been felled, a sign that there were people somewhere at no great distance off. We walked a mile or two, in several directions, in the hopes of discovering a village, but were disappointed; and again in the evening we had no success in our search after game, not even a partridge being found. We went to bed in something approaching a bad humour. The monotonous solitude of this place does not agree with us.

Dec. 7.—The scenery of some parts of the country is very beautiful, but the absence of mountains, and even hills, gives it a somewhat monotonous appearance. Since we have been in the country we have scarcely seen a mound or hillock, and nothing whatever in the shape of a range or chain of hills. The highest ground we have crossed I should imagine is not more than two hundred feet above sea level. But everywhere the forest scenery is very diversified, and the beauty of the flowers, especially the creepers, beyond all description.

We made two marches to-day, one in the morning, the other late in the afternoon. As we were crossing a small plain towards evening, three rhinoceroses came in sight; but though we galloped after them full speed, we could not get near enough for a shot. In places where the country is not so thickly wooded, there are abundance of wild plum trees. The fruit is equal in flavour and larger in size than that obtained in Europe. We also met with peaches and apricots. In the morning a village was seen, but not entered, as it lay out of our road.

DEC. 8.—Very shortly after resuming our journey, we came within sight of large tracts of cultivated ground, and two villages, besides many scattered huts and several pagodas. These latter were situated apart from the dwellings, and surrounded by magnificent banyan trees, under which sat several Buddhist priests at their devotions, and some of those Eastern fanatics who show their zeal for religion by distorting their bodies into various eccentric and painful positions. As we passed we threw them a few small coins, which were picked up by the boys in attendance upon them. One of the pagodas was a very large and fine building, and there seemed to be a great many priests about it. The dome and minaret, as in all similar buildings we saw in Siam, were highly ornamented and covered with gilt.

Upon passing the first village, though considerable curiosity was excited, the inhabitants did not pay that attention to us we had experienced in places farther to the west. So many Chinese, Anamese, &c., were seen, that we felt certain we were approaching Lahaing; and on stopping to make inquiries were assured that that city might be reached by a person on foot in five hours. From this we concluded it to be fifteen miles distant—rather a long march for the oxen; but we determined to attempt to reach it to-day. The people with whom we communicated were obliging and civil, and great order appeared to be maintained amongst themselves. The street of the village was full of the covered stalls of native and Chinese* merchants; and there was a great deal of trade going on, considering the small size of the place.

With temporary halts, we continued our march the greater part of the day, passing through three villages, one of which might almost be called a town. Many other villages were seen on our right and left hand, and the country is highly cultivated. We were much surprised to find the country so thickly populated, while twenty miles to the westward not an inhabitant was to be seen.

Five o'clock in the afternoon.—In sight of Lahaing. It looks like a large city, its

* The number of Chinese, Anamese, Savs, Malays, and other foreigners, settled in this country is almost incredible.

7

minarets forming a complete forest. We arrive on the right bank of the Menam, and halt, the cattle being thoroughly exhausted, having covered more than twenty miles during the day. There is a great similarity in the appearance of the Siamese cities. Houses on piles, thousands of domes and minarets, mud, water, floating streets, a crowd whose noise is deafening, and bustle confusing, fancifully decorated pagodas, and splendid palaces of the rajahs—imagine this, and that the surging crowd is dressed in every form and colour of Eastern costume, and you have a Siamese city, at least, so far as it can be conceived without being seen. At Lahaing, as at Bangkok and other cities of the Siamese empire, the greatest part of the town is built on rafts which float in the river. These rafts are constructed of timber, and each carry from one to twenty houses, according to size. I think it probable that these raft-houses were first introduced into the country by the Chinese. However that may be, these people are the principal inhabitants of them at Lahaing, the natives preferring the pile dwellings; and all the chiefs' houses and pagodas, as well as many other buildings, being built on the solid ground on the left bank of the river, where they are very liable to be flooded, and, indeed, are abandoned by most of the inhabitants during the rainy season.

DEC. 9.—Throughout this day we were busy in getting the oxen, horses, and baggage ferried across the Menam; a job that was not only very troublesome, but occupied a long time, owing to the width and crowded state of the river. On the opposite shore we took ground a mile outside the city, and a little inland from the river. We did not attempt to procure a native house or lodgings, having found by experience that we were more comfortable in our own tent. We were much pestered by Chinese and native pedlars, who tried to force their wares upon us. Lahaing is an exceedingly busy and bustling place, though we do not think the permanent population can exceed ten or twelve thousand, of whom quite three-fourths are foreigners (Chinese, &c.), not born in the country. The bazaar is large, and almost any description of goods can be procured there, including many European articles.

Dec. 10.—While walking in the city we saw a caravan, consisting of nearly two hundred elephants, laden with merchandise, start on their journey towards the north. It was an interesting and imposing sight to witness so many of the huge beasts together, and all under the most perfect control. We made many inquiries as to the destination of this caravan, but could gain no information on the subject; neither could we learn what kind of merchandise it was carrying, though we found out that a few of the elephants were laden with ivory. We were pretty confident that the natives could have given us all the information we desired about these merchants; but they delight in raising mysteries about their trading transactions, even when there is not the slightest advantage to be gained by so doing.

We did not see a single horse at Lahaing, and ours were objects of great curiosity to the inhabitants. Neither were many oxen used as beasts of burden; but there was a great number of elephants to be seen in all parts of the city and its neighbourhood. There are scarcely any domestic animals kept by the people, except pigs and dogs and great numbers of fowls. The pigs are kept amongst the houses, and allowed to run about the streets, and from this and other causes the stench in some parts of the city is insupportable. The dogs are also a great nuisance, as every now and then they take it into their heads to follow foot passengers in packs, snarling and barking and making one shake for his shins; yet, as they are of great use in helping to eat up the offal and filth of the city, you must not kill or molest them. But the principal scavengers are the hawks or kites, which are as numerous on the housetops as sparrows in England. As soon as any remnant of food is thrown out, one or more of these birds will pounce upon it almost before it touches the ground; indeed, if you throw a piece of meat into the air, it is sure to be caught in the talons of one of the birds before it descends. They frequently snatch the meat from the dishes as they are carried along by the servants, and in Bengal I have seen the soldiers amusing themselves with a rather cruel sport: they spread a blanket on the ground upon which a bone or bit of meat is placed. Down darts a kite, and in snatching at the bait its claws (they always seize their prey with their talons) catch in the blanket, and as they will not release their hold very readily, it may be enveloped in the blanket with ease, and so captured. Pieces of paper and rag are then tied to its tail, and it is set at liberty. Its companions at once set upon it, and after a short contest tear it to pieces.

Speaking of this, reminds me to say that the Siamese are great cock-fighters. These birds are large, with strong legs, and fight desperately; but I don't think any betting takes place amongst those who thus amuse themselves; neither do they usually affix artificial spurs to the birds: indeed, I do not know certainly whether they ever do.

We bought some very ingeniously carved soap-stone ornaments at Lahaing, but I cannot say whether they were of native workmanship or not. The Siamese, from whom we bought them, declared they were; but a native merchant's word is not worth much. It is quite likely that they were the work of a Chinaman, but if so, were executed with more than ordinary skill. One of these ornaments represented a ship lying off a rocky coast with trees. The trees and the spars and ropes of the ship were cut out with marvellous delicacy. Another piece represented a grove of cocoa-nut trees, and a third, a group of native men and women. This last was curious, but the forms and features of the figures were not well executed, and the artist evidently excelled in carving inanimate objects.

In the evening, a travelling conjurer passed our tent. At sight of us he stopped and prepared to give an exhibition. While he was spreading out a white cloth on the ground and arranging the contents of a small box which he carried with him, a crowd of natives collected around, squatting on their heels, in anticipation of the amusement. While the conjurer was still pretending to search amongst the articles in his box, a small snake crept from under the cloth which he had spread upon the ground, and we, imagining it had come there by accident, seized a stick, with the intention of destroying it; but the man took it up and deliberately swallowed it head first. That he actually swallowed it, I, of course, do not believe; but it could be distinctly seen slowly slipping down his throat, and in whatever way our eyes were deceived, this man was marvellously clever. While we were still staring at him in blank astonishment, and expecting to see him pull the serpent up his throat again, a dozen small birds appeared upon the cloth, and after hopping about, and going through the motions of picking up food, flew, one by one, into a bag which the man held out, and disappeared. He afterwards squeezed the bag, and flattened it out to prove that the birds were not there. These birds were evidently cleverly constructed models, but about the snake we could not agree, Mr. Grant being of opinion that it was really a live snake, and it certainly had the appearance of being such. It was of the common harmless green species, and about eighteen inches in length.

After going through a few commonplace tricks, such as every one who has been in India has seen, the conjurer suddenly caused his cloth to be covered with beautifully coloured insects, such as butterflies, beetles, grasshoppers, &c., which all moved about as though possessed of life, though there was, at least, a hundred of them. The greatest mystery about these tricks was how the creatures got upon the cloth. They were there in an instant, and although we watched the man closely and carefully, we could not say whether they fell from his hand, came from above, or crept from underneath the cloth. They seemed to appear spontaneously, and disappeared in the same way.

After this, the man performed a trick similar to that known in England as the Japanese butterfly trick, only he used a feather instead of a fly. Sending the feather up to about six feet above his head, he fixed his eyes intently upon it, and without apparently exercising any other influence upon it, caused it to whirl round in a spiral direction, to dart suddenly up into the air, to descend with the rapidity of a stone, and to perform other strange antics. He next, without our having observed him put anything into his mouth, spat out some liquid which was first of a crimson colour, then green, blue, lilac, yellow, &c., in succession. Lastly, he opened his mouth and showed it to be full of fire. After spitting out jets of fire in every direction, he spoke some words to the cloth, and it rolled up of itself like a linen blind that is drawn with cords. Before packing up his box, he presented a small wooden cup to each individual of the crowd, who had appeared to enjoy themselves immensely, giving vent to loud shouts and peals of laughter at the conclusion of each trick. We ourselves were so pleased with what we had seen, that when the cup was placed before us, we dropped two rupees into it, at which the man seemed almost overjoyed. Shouldering his box and bag, he made an obeisance, and wended his way towards Lahaing.

We were much tormented during the night by swarms of musquitos, which came from the river, and by the intrusion upon our privacy of certain large lizards. These latter gentlemen kept constantly bringing their cold bodies in conjunction with my flesh, as I lay in bed; and my decided repugnance to such a proceeding was a source of great amusement to Messrs. Lacy and Grant, who were not so sensitive in this matter as myself. When at length I fell asleep, I had horrifying dreams of conjurers who dealt in the black art, and brought into existence frightful-looking salamanders, as large as mountains. It was broad daylight when I awoke, and Grant and Lacy were already up, and making preparations for the resumption of our journey: for it had been decided that we should leave Lahaing to-day.

CHAPTER VI.

Hot day.—River Menam.—Parties of natives met.—Dense forest.—Pea-fowl shooting.—An aquatic village.—Marshy ground.—A tiger wounded.—Two buffaloes shot.—A sporting expedition.—Inundated tracts of country.—Numerous traces of game.—A herd of large deer.—Magnificent banyan trees.—A solitary rhinoceros seen, and shortly afterwards find others.—One of them placed *hors de combat*.—Damage done to crops by rhinoceroses and other wild beasts.—Cowardice displayed by tigers.—Several shot by ourselves and servants.—Magnificent display of fireflies.—These insects preyed upon by a small kind of hawk.—Boggy nature of the country.—Excessive heat.

Dec. 11.—It was very hot during the morning, the thermometer registering 97° in the shade; we did not, consequently, leave our ground until four o'clock in the afternoon, when the heat had somewhat modified. Our course was now nearly due south, along the left bank of the Menam, which is a magnificent river, and one of the finest in Farther India. It has a course of about eight hundred miles, and its native name signifies "The Mother of Waters." It has a breadth, just below La-haing, of fully three-quarters of a mile; but the current is slow, and there are some small islets in mid-stream, upon which houses have been built. The surface of the water is completely covered with floating houses, boats, barges, and rafts; and a large trade is carried on by means of the communication this river affords with Bangkok, and other places down the stream.

After wending our way for a short distance amongst the huts erected close to the brink of the river, we found the ground so overgrown with rank grass and plants, that we were compelled to choose our road farther inland, where the trees were tall, with straight trunks, and the ground between them free from undergrowth. As we advanced the trees grew more thickly together, and whenever we caught a glimpse of the river, we perceived that the other bank also was clothed with a thick forest-growth: nevertheless, some considerable patches had been cleared of timber, and turned into prosperous maize-fields, in the neighbourhood of which we passed by one or two small hamlets. A great many natives were met on the road, carrying grain to Lahaing in baskets.

DEC. 12.—Found the ground difficult to get over on account of the long grass and tangled herbage with which it was covered. We were also delayed through one of the oxen falling lame. In the space of seven miles we found two villages, and passed through them both, passing the remainder of the day and the night in one of them; but nothing occurred of sufficient interest to be noted. We heard some terrible tales about tigers, which we were assured were very numerous about here.

DEC. 13.—Dense forest clothes both banks of the river down to the water's edge, and it is full of monkeys, and birds of many different sorts, particularly parrots and pigeons, and pea-fowl. We have several times previously met with odd individuals of the latter bird, but here they seem to be abundant; and when we had finished our allotted day's journey and partaken of dinner, we wandered off into the forest for a little sport with them. They are difficult things to shoot, for being large birds they will carry a lot of shot, especially as they keep near the tops of the trees, and can seldom be hit strongly. Yet, notwithstanding these drawbacks, I like pea-fowl shooting better than any other sport amongst small game, and it is not without a little excitement. You wander off into the most gloomy parts of the forest alone; for if two or three persons went together it would spoil the chance of making a good bag, owing to the wariness of the birds. The ground is covered with luxuriant undergrowth, which is tall and thick enough to almost entirely conceal you from view, and the light is so subdued that there is little chance of the birds discovering you if you are careful to avoid making too much noise. Above, however, the light shines through the branches of the trees, and you can see the magnificent birds plainly, their gorgeous tails elevated, and the rays of the sun playing upon them, and showing off in full advantage all their charming variegations. The foliage is so thick, that it is some time before you get a clear aim, but at last you fire. You look anxiously for the fall of the bird, but a horrible screech grates on your ear and away go the pea-fowl. You hope for better success next time, and working your way laboriously through the brushwood, come presently to a tall tree in which are several nests of enormous size. The birds have heard your approach, and are gone; but you keep quiet, and in a few minutes two or three of them fly heavily back to their nests. The report of the gun rattles and echoes through the forest noisily, and the bird chancing to be hit in a vital spot, drops like a stone, and crashes into the jungle below. You secure it quickly, for if any life is left in it, it will run with great rapidity, and as you cannot follow it through the thick undergrowth, it will certainly be lost. The next shot is also successful, so far as killing the bird goes; but the branches are so thick above that in its fall it lodges amongst them, and of course cannot be got at. It is a long time, before you get another shot, and then the bird is only wounded, and flutters away uttering its piercing cry. You are fortunate if you secure one in every four you hit. After four hours' shooting, we had only nine birds to show amongst the three of us.

DEC. 14.—We passed a large village to-day, built almost entirely in the river, partly upon large piles and partly upon floating rafts. Several pagodas belonging to this village were built in the forest a short distance from the river.

Dec. 15.—The ground near the river was so marshy, that we consumed six hours in floundering ten miles. Mr. Grant and one of the servants went about eight miles to the east away from the river, but found no change in the character of the country. They brought in half a dozen pea-fowl, some partridges, and a small antelope, which Mr. Grant had shot. He had also seen a large tiger, but it had refused to show fight, and in spite of his efforts got away, though wounded.

We saw a village on the opposite bank of the river, distant about three miles, and a fleet of twenty-nine trading boats and rafts, manned by Chinese and natives, passed us going down the river. They were propelling themselves with long poles.

In the evening we surprised a herd of between fifty and sixty buffalo wallowing in the mud on the river's bank. Two of them fell before our rifles, and afforded us the great luxury of a little fresh beef. A short time after the slaughter of these buffalo, two tigers were seen lurking about on the skirts of the forest, attracted, probably, by the smell of the blood. Before we could load our rifles and come up with them, they disappeared; and although we searched the neighbourhood thoroughly, nothing more was seen of them. These circumstances led us to suppose that game was plentiful in this tract of country, and the following day was devoted to a hunting expedition.

Our sporting party was ready for action and fell in at half-past four in the morning. It consisted of our three selves, and two of the men, the rest of our party being left behind with the oxen and baggage, with orders to remain stationary and keep a sharp look-out for tigers, which we thought might be attracted by the cattle, and especially the horses: for all tigers have a strong predilection for human and horse-flesh. Captain Lacy's servant, Akbar Nanee, a steady man, was left in charge of our camp. We carried with us a supply of cooked buffalo-flesh and other provisions, and also our cloaks and blankets in case we should find it necessary to pass the night away from our wandering home.

After marching three or four miles in a north-easterly direction, we were stopped by the condition of the ground, which was so boggy as to be dangerous. Large tracts of the forest-ground was under water, which had doubtless collected during the rainy season and not yet evaporated. We changed our course to south-east, and at last to due east; but in every direction the ground was so sodden that we were more than ankle-deep in mud. Numerous footprints of buffalo, deer, and rhinoceroses were seen, and also traces of the elephant, tiger, and some unknown animal. We saw a number of buffalo in the river, with only just their noses showing above water; but they were in such a position that we could not get at them. We might, indeed, have shot them at long range, but as this would have been a wanton slaughter from which we could not reap the least advantage we refrained from firing.

The first game we fell in with, at about half-past eight o'clock, was a species of deer, not hitherto met with. It was a sort of roebuck, considerably larger than the antelopes with which most parts of the country abound. A large herd of these was discovered grazing upon some slightly elevated ground ; which was, in consequence, much drier than the surrounding country. Both bucks and does were furnished with horns, but those of the former were much the finest; and the bucks were also much the largest animals, even more so than in most of the species of the deer tribe. We fired upon them, and one of the largest bucks leaped seven or eight feet into the air as though electrified before it fell and died. Two others showed signs of being badly wounded, and one of them only ran three or four hundred yards before it fell; but the other got away. We followed its blood-marked track until it was lost in a miry morass where we dared not venture. After securing the best parts of those which had fallen into our hands, we resumed our way eastward, and soon found the ground more firm; and some parts that were quite dry. There were, however, still large shallow pools, or rather tracks of inundated land, which were so densely covered with trees and jungle growth, that we could not form much idea of their actual extent. All the trees in this moist region are very large and fine, and most of them quite two hundred feet in height. They are full of those ubiquitous parrots which we seem to find in every creek and corner of the country; but there are not many monkeys here, and those of a small kind. Pea-fowl are tolerably numerous, but they are shy, and keep at the tops of the trees, where small shot will not reach them with effect.

About ten o'clock we selected a spot for preparing our dinner and passing the day, there being no chance of meeting with game now until evening. A fine banyan tree, covering at least an acre of ground, answered our purpose admirably. It is well known that these trees throw out shoots from above which take root when they reach the ground, and become trees in themselves though still attached to the parent trunk; thus in time a single tree becomes a complete grove, affording the completest and most delightful shades from the heat that is to be found in the excessively hot climates where it grows. This is one reason, doubtless, why the tree has come to be held sacred by the Indians. A single tree has frequently many hundreds of these trunks, which look very much like artificial props placed to support the branches. The amount of animal life that harbours in trees of this genus is astonishing. Mr. Grant, who was making a magnificent collection of insects, assured me that he had found as many as one hundred and sixty-seven different species of beetles on the banyan tree alone; and the thousands of birds that breed amidst its thick foliage, could not, I am sure, be described in one volume.

We had wandered a long way from our camp: so far, that if we intended to return there to pass the night, and it was very desirable that we should do so, it would be necessary for us to start early in the afternoon, especially as we intended to move in a circuitous direction with the object of examining as wide a tract of country as possible for the game of which we were in search. Accordingly, we left the shade of our banyan about three in the afternoon, though the heat was then at its height. Our march was a tiresome one, owing to the detours we were constantly obliged to make in order to avoid the numerous bogs and morasses which abounded. That all sorts of large game was abundant, was evidenced by the footmarks which were met with at every pace; but we saw none until nearly seven o'clock in the evening, at which time we concluded ourselves to be distant from our camp about nine miles. About this time a solitary rhinoceros was seen, and, as was the case with other animals of this kind on a former occasion, it took fright long before we could get near enough to attack it. Very shortly afterwards, however, a small herd of five rhinoceroses came right across our path, and received our fire from a distance of about ninety yards. None of the herd fell, but one creature was wounded in the right fore leg so severely that the limb was rendered useless; and, of course, the animal could not follow its companions, who made off at a gallop. Our friend, however, made the best use of his three remaining legs, and on our approach to finish him off, made a most determined effort to charge, lowering his formidable-looking horns, and advancing on his three pins quickly enough to make it necessary for us to display some activity in getting out of his way. He was shot down without much difficulty, taking seven bullets into his podgy carcass before he went down upon his knees and yielded up the ghost. It was a fine animal, but not so large as some we afterwards met with. The rhinoceroses, as well as elephants and buffalo, in this country often nearly ruin the villagers by breaking into the rice and maize fields, and beating down the grain with the weight of their huge bodies: for they destroy, at least, twenty times as much as they eat. The only methods they usually resort to to destroy them are pitfalls, but some of the rajahs and chiefs hunt them for sport, invariably shooting them, like tigers, from elephant-back.

As we approached our camp we saw several tigers, probably the same that had been seen the previous evening. That they were attracted by the presence of our cattle there could be little doubt. They were cowardly, and tried in each case to get away. One fellow got a shot through the loins that stopped him, and although he showed his teeth, with a great deal of horrid growling, he had not much pluck in him, and was easily killed. We found upon reaching our tent that Akbar had also seen tigers lurking about, as on last evening, and, assisted by Laoo and the other servants, had succeeded in shooting one and driving the others away. A country in which these dangerous beasts are so numerous can scarcely be called agreeable, notwithstanding the beauty of the scenery.

After dark myriads of fire-flies appeared about the trees, and a more grand and astonishing sight I have never witnessed. The whole forest seemed to be full of brilliant lamps, showing a silver-coloured light. Suddenly every light would be extinguished, and after an interval of a few seconds would simultaneously recommence shining again. It may easily be conceived what an extraordinary effect this would have. Fancy an immense forest of gigantic trees, illumináted with innumerable thousands of bright lights, and these lights disappearing and reappearing at regular intervals, perhaps seven or eight times a minute, and you have some vague notion of the grand sight that met our gaze in this part of the Siamese Empire. The light emitted by these flies is very different from and much more brilliant than that of the glow-worms met with in Europe, and the insect itself is of considerable size. They seemed to be stationary while showing their light regularly together; but amongst the sedge by the river a few were dancing about, and the phosphorescence of these continued to shine with a steady glow, and was not extinguished at intervals like that of those on the trees. They continued shining throughout the night. It is not satisfactorily known for what purpose these insects emit this glow. Some think it is to light them in their search for prey, others that it is to attract the male insect; for only the females have the power of thus shining. I think it must be to attract their prey to them, for it is well known how quickly nocturnal insects (upon which the fire-fly feeds) will cluster round anything bright or emitting a light. But it also serves to guide their enemies toward them, for we discovered that lizards and several kinds of night-birds prey upon them. They were particularly sought after by a small hawk, one of which we shot, and found the stomach full of the fire-flies. The bird was less in size than a pigeon, and prettily and curiously marked with different shades, brown, black, and a little white. Mr. Grant cured the skin, with the intention, I believe, of sending it to some natural history society in Europe when our travels should be finished.

Dec. 17.—It is evident that we shall not be able to advance much farther along the banks of the river, on account of the very swampy state of the ground; and after a consultation, we decided to move eastward until we should find higher and drier ground. A twelve-mile march brought us to a more comfortable tract of land, but there is still a great quantity of moisture and mud on all sides; and the character of the forest is in nowise altered. I think I have forgotten to say that there is an absence of creepers and parasitical plants on the trees in this region; but the undergrowth is very rank, and there are many large and coarse, but gaudy-looking, flowers. Some of the shrubs, also, are covered with clusters of handsome blossom, having a faint, pleasant smell. No snakes have been seen amongst these morasses, nor alligators in the river, though we have heard it reported that they are found there. This country is probably too moist for the serpent tribes. In the evening we shot a deer and a few pea-fowl.

Dec. 18.—A warm, close, and fatiguing day. We marched about fourteen miles in all, halting frequently to rest ourselves and the cattle. A herd of wild elephants was passed about the middle of the day, enjoying themselves in a muddy pool. We did not molest them; but in the evening a prowling tiger was dealt with less mercifully, and Captain Lacy killed it with a single shot, which penetrated the creature's brain. Plenty of wild fruit trees grow here, and afford us a pleasant means of cooling our parched throats; for the thermometer stands at 107° in the shade, a degree of heat which I believe is rare in this country, at least at this season of the year.

Dec. 19.—The face of the country is covered with an almost unbroken forest, with trees full two hundred feet in height; but the ground is dry, scarcely a moist place being now discernible. We can see no traces of inhabitants in these parts.

CHAPTER VII.

Pace of the oxen.—Range of hills.—Character of the country.—Monkeys, and a free fight amongst them.—Wild bees' nests.—Ruins of a pagoda.—Wells.—Storms of hail and rain.—Trees found in this region.—Stream and lotus flowers.—Cultivated land.—Village or town of Tatsong. —Rajah of Tatsong.—Description of the place.—The Rajah's palace.—Courteous reception by the Rajah.—His personal appearance.—Subjects of our conversation.—His territory.—A tiger hunt proposed.—In the howdah.— The sport commences.—Timidity of the beaters.—Character of the tiger.—A desperate encounter.—A native saved by his elephant.—Result of our day's sport.

DECEMBER 20.—Having passed the night near a small stream which runs towards the Menam, and probably empties itself into that river, we resumed our journey a little after eight o'clock. The forest was too close and the undergrowth too thick to admit of our advancing very rapidly (I use the word rapidly advisedly, since the oxen, under the best of circumstances, never cover more than three miles an hour), but in a couple of hours or so we came to a ridge of hills— the first we had met with in the country. Though not more than four or five hundred feet in height they were steep and covered with wood; and we were obliged to dismount and lead our horses. By the time we had reached the ridge of these hills the perspiration was running from us freely, and we were glad to make a halt. This range of hills appeared to run due north and south, but we could not trace it with the eye very far in either direction. These hills had not been visible before on account of the density of the forest, which had continually prevented our having an extended view in any direction. From our present elevated stand, however, we could see several low hills, some of them isolated, others running in low broken chains north and south, and none of them exceeding two or three hundred feet in height. Indeed, the country (and we could see a long distance with the aid of our glasses) was not nearly so hilly as the county of Surrey in England, though some of the ranges were very steep, being, in fact, cliffs, and all densely wooded, and presenting a rugged and romantic appearance.

In the flat, level country lying to the north-east we saw a number of slender spiral minarets peeping up from amidst the trees. Supposing there was a village at this spot, we did not prolong our halt unnecessarily; but as soon as the cattle and ourselves were sufficiently rested, proceeded towards these minarets, which were seven or eight miles distant, and only visible through a glass. So thickly was the country wooded that we were compelled to have recourse to a compass for guidance, and the undergrowth and ground creepers were so troublesome that frequently the oxen could scarcely force a passage. In this forest there were a great many monkeys of three different species. We had not seen any for several days previously. One kind was very large and like a baboon, except that it had a tail; the other species were both small, one being a variety of the spider-monkey, the other the small kind most commonly met with in every part of the country hitherto passed through. These monkeys were quarrelsome amongst themselves, and we witnessed several battles between the two smaller species, in which they fought desperately, using their teeth and nails, and making a tremendous chattering. Where large parties of them were fighting, the trees presented a curious spectacle, the branches shaking violently, and showers of leaves falling, and we picked up several dead combatants who had been torn nearly to pieces. The rage of these little creatures was ludicrous to behold ; they screamed with excitement, rushed from branch to branch so quickly that the eye could scarcely follow them, and performed the strangest antics, apparently indicative of their defiance and hatred of the foe. The contest did not cease until one party or the other had been driven from the tree, the exclusive possession of which seemed to be the bone of contention.

The nests of wild bees were very abundant in this forest, being found in almost every decayed tree. We obtained plenty of honey, but not without some trouble and a sting or two. The bees are very much enraged when disturbed, and if you do not make a great smoke, will attack you dangerously about the face and head. We found the best way of driving them out of their nests was to insert a little wet powder, which stupefied them for the time, and gave us an opportunity of getting safely away with the plunder.

After more than four hours' hard marching over distressing ground, we arrived at the site of our hoped-for village. It turned out, however, to be merely the ruins of a large pagoda or idol-temple. It was quite deserted, and the walls partly broken down. A grove of banyan trees surrounded it, and many of the trunks or root-like branches which grow perpendicularly downwards from the boughs of this tree, had forced themselves through the roof and taken root in the interior of the building, which was nearly choked up with ferns, creepers, thorns and grass, which afforded harbourage to innumerable lizards and small snakes. A colony of storks had also built their nests on the roof and dome of the decayed building, which was square in shape, and about a hundred and sixty feet in length and breadth. The interior had, at one time, been divided into six compartments; but the partitions had been broken down, the idols removed, and the flooring torn up. The walls had been covered with some sort of plaster, handsomely painted in various curious and fantastic devices. The stone pillars which supported the roof were covered with rude representations of elephants, rhinoceroses, boars, serpents and birds. In places precious stones seemed to have been embedded in the plaster, and we found a few rubies of inferior value still sticking in it. We picked them out and brought them away, but they were useless except as curiosities. Former visitors to the place had probably taken away all that was valuable.

In the courtyard at the back of the temple was a deep well with a stone parapet round it. We obtained some deliciously cool water from it. All that remained of the wall which had once enclosed this courtyard, was a heap of rubbish and large rough-hewn stones. The dome of the pagoda was still in tolerably good repair, and thirty-seven minarets remained, though many were broken and lying on the ground. The age of this temple it was impossible to conjecture, for neither of us was very deeply versed in archæology; but it was undoubtedly at least several hundred years old, for it looked as if it had been abandoned for centuries. In its neighbourhood we discovered other ruins, apparently of large stone buildings; but whether these had been religious edifices or not I cannot say. In the forest surrounding them there were other traces that a village or town had once stood upon this spot. The night was passed under the walls of the pagoda. About midnight we had a tremendous storm: the rain, mixed with large hail-stones, came down in torrents, soaking through our tent and wetting us to the skin. The lightning was incessant and exceedingly brilliant, and the peals of thunder deafening. Lightning and thunder are of almost nightly occurrence in this, and all warm countries; but this is the first rain that has fallen since the commencement of our journey.

DEC. 21.—We were on the march early this morning, moving in a south-east course. Forest covers the country in every direction, and the ground is mostly flat; though here and there we cross a hill. Abundant traces of game are observable, but it either moves out of the way alarmed at our approach, or from some other reason keeps out of sight; for, with the exception of a single rhinoceros, no animal was seen.

In the forests cocoa-nut trees, fig-trees, wild plums and peaches, sandal-wood, teak, betel-nut palms, and scores of, to us, unknown trees were seen. Besides these, gigantic bamboos, canes, and other plants of the same nature grew in impenetrable brakes, many of them adorned with most beautiful foliage. Here, also, we again met with the creepers and parasitical plants in great profusion.

We broke our march, performing part in the morning and part in the evening. The whole distance covered was about sixteen miles, in a south and south-east direction. Our halting-place was on the right bank of a stream about twenty yards wide, the surface of which was completely covered with lotus flowers, some pure white in colour, others of a red hue.

DEC. 22.—Notwithstanding the small width of the brook, we found there were seven or eight feet of water in it in most places; and much time was lost before we could find a fordable place. After keeping in a south slightly west direction (we being anxious to make the banks of the Menam again) for ten miles, we sighted a large village lying three miles west of us. Towards this village we wended our way, and arrived there in something less than an hour. The last mile of our journey was through rice-fields—the only grain we found grown here; but there were large gardens in and immediately round the place, where melons, pumpkins, vegetables and fruits of all kinds were cultivated in vast quantities.

The reception we met with here was in marked contrast to that accorded us in most places we had passed through. The inhabitants did not betray the least curiosity about us or our business, and though a small crowd of children assembled when we began to erect our tent, near the centre of the village, scarcely an adult was seen. When we walked through the village—the streets of which were arranged like the rays of a star, meeting in the middle—the women peeped at us through the doorways, and a pack of unmannerly dogs yelped at our heels; but otherwise we did not attract any attention. We soon learned, however, that our presence was not altogether unnoticed, even in high quarters; for about five o'clock in the afternoon a messenger came to us from the Rajah or chief magistrate of Tatsong, as the village was called, to make inquiries as to who we were and what we wanted. We replied that we were Englishmen from India, and were travelling through the country for pleasure and to shoot the wild animals. In about an hour the messengers returned with an intimation that the Rajah* would like to see us, and of course we went at once, taking Angbang, our interpreter, with us.

* I call him Rajah (that is a king) because, as will be seen presently, he had almost independent power in this district, and I could not distinctly ascertain his native title. He appeared to be known by many various titles.

The houses of the village or rather town (for it is a place of considerable size) of Tatsong are large and substantially built, though constructed almost entirely of timber. They are arranged in few straggling streets which all shoot out from a large open space in the centre of the town. It was in this open space that we had pitched our tent, and it was also occupied by a few huts, and shaded by an enormous banyan tree and some palms. Many of the houses were built under the shade of banyans, which had shot their tributary trunks down into the middle of the road; so that one of the streets, a quarter of a mile in length, was completely canopied over with an arch of foliage, which looked as if supported by rough wooden props, presenting a most singular sight, which I am quite at a loss to describe. The other streets had rows of fig-trees and palms planted in them, but not arranged in regular order; as some were growing close into the houses, and others in the middle of the roadway. Altogether this is the prettiest and most picturesque town I have seen in any eastern country. There are no less than seventeen pagodas in it or its immediate neighbourhood, though all of small size, and not so handsome as some we have seen in other districts. There are a great many wells of water in the roads, to which the inhabitants come for water for domestic use. The palace of the Rajah is situated at the north end of the town, and quite outside of it. It is a large building of oblong shape, and built upon a raised terrace of masonry. Its appearance is rather heavy and prison-like, though it is highly ornamented with sculptures in relievo over the whole façade, representing the animals and birds found in the country; as well as human figures, flowers, ornamental devices, &c. The main entrance is wide and lofty, and accessible by a flight of stone steps, eighty-nine in number. On either side of the gateway is a gigantic carved figure, and inside two others, facing in an opposite direction to the first. The courtyard is about two hundred yards in length by eighty broad, and the palace proper is on the west side of it.

The most remarkable feature in the architecture of the palace is the windows, some of which project forward from the wall with balconies in front, and penthouse to protect them from the sun and weather, and others raised inwards. All of them are closed with lattice-work and painted blinds; but they have no substitute for glass, or contrivances, beside those mentioned, for keeping out the wind and rain. The roof is flat, and used as a promenade. The whole upper part of the building is constructed of brick, but there is much granite-like stone about the foundation; and the images, &c., are carved out of stone of this kind. In the interior, those rooms into which we had the privilege of entering were large and lofty, the ceilings and walls being covered with painted plaster. Much labour must have been expended upon the devices, which mostly represented flowers, birds, men and trees. In one apartment there was a rude attempt at a landscape, but it was scarcely intelligible.

Upon arriving at the place, we were taken by a score of servants into the Rajah's presence.

His Highness sat upon the floor, which was covered with a showy carpet of good texture, and apparently of Persian manufacture. The small crowd of attendants which had shown us in, remained outside the doorway; and there were only five head attendants, or chiefs, standing round the Rajah, who courteously invited us to sit, and we squatted cross-legged on the floor, with our interpreter standing between us.

The Rajah was a small man, with pleasant features, and a good-humoured smile habitually playing about his mouth. He spoke with vivacity, and, from the nature of the questions he put to us and his whole manner and appearance, I should say he was a man of great intellectual power. His age was about forty years. He wore a rather gorgeous embroidered dress, and was adorned with great quantities of jewellery, his fingers being covered with rings, and his breast with a kind of diamond breastplate of immense value. The apartment in which he was sitting was quite destitute of furniture, the only articles in it being carpets, mats, fans, pipes, and a few ornamental trifles. Both the Rajah and his attendants were armed with jewelled swords and daggers, and the Rajah had an elegant pair of pistols in his girdle.

Our interview lasted nearly two hours, and our conversation—maintained, of course, through the interpreter—extended over a great variety of subjects; for the Rajah wanted to know all about ourselves and our country, how long we had been in Siam, where we were going, what we thought of his people, how the English governed in India and in England, and hundreds of other questions of a similar nature. He had been to Bangkok several times, he said, and seen English and other Europeans there. On one occasion he had seen a large war-ship there, and declared it was one of the most wonderful sights he had seen. He had heard a great deal about the English, and knew they were a mighty people, and was very pleased to see some of them in his country. He thought we were the only Europeans who ever passed through Tatsong, and was sure none had been there in his life-time.

We learned now and on subsequent occasions, that the Rajah had absolute authority in his own district, but paid a tribute to the King of Siam. The exact dimensions of the district he governed we could not determine. The Rajah told us, however, that it contained twenty-three villages, of which Tatsong is the principal, and gives its name to the entire territory. The population do not cultivate any produce save rice; but they trade to Bangkok with elephant's tusks, betel-nuts, honey, pepper, wax, and palm-oil.

The Rajah's name is Shangar Dee, as we learnt from one of his attendants. He was much amused with the accounts of hunting adventures which we related at his desire, assured us he was himself a sportsman, and invited us to join him in a tiger hunt. He also graciously inquired where we were lodging, and said we might occupy a portion of his palace if we would like to do so; but this kind offer we declined, preferring to remain in our own tent where we should feel we had more liberty of action. When we took our leave, his Highness got upon his legs and shook hands with each one of us very cordially, and reminded us that it would be necessary to start early on our hunting expedition the forthcoming day. We assured him we should be ready by the appointed hour, and left the palace, accompanied by several of the Rajah's attendants, who, by command of their master, conducted us back to our tent.

DEC. 23.—Between five and six o'clock this morning, some twenty of the Rajah's servants came to escort us to the palace. Arriving there we found the Rajah ready, with four elephants, it being intended that we should hunt from elephant-back. Captain Lacy mounted into the Rajah's howdah, myself and Mr. Grant into those of two of the attending chiefs; the fourth howdah was occupied exclusively by native chiefs or heads of the Rajah's household.

My companions, five in number, were all of them officers of the Rajah; and one was related to him. Having no interpreter, I could not hold any conversation with them, and I felt sorry myself and two fellow-travellers had not been placed in the same howdah, which would have materially increased the enjoyment of the day.

The motion of riding on elephant-back is steady and pleasant, and it is a far better method of travelling than in palanquins or on horse-back. The elephants move quickly, and are as sure-footed as a mule. I never heard of one making a false step; and yet they will descend hills where a horse would be almost sure to stumble. They overcome all obstacles that lie in the road, crushing through jungle that would be quite impenetrable to man or horse, and swimming across the broadest rivers with perfect ease, and safety to the occupants of the howdah.

Two or three hundred of the male part of the population of Tatsong accompanied the elephants on foot to act as beaters. They were armed with long sticks and spears, and acted under the direction of leaders, who placed them in position when we arrived on the hunting-ground. They formed themselves into a crescent or half-moon, and closed in gradually on the patches of jungle, driving out all the game in our direction.

Deer and antelope were the only animals met with for some hours, and of these more than a score were shot from the four howdahs, the Rajah bringing down seven with his own hand. In drawing some of the wildest tracts of jungle, two leopards and a tiger were started, and speedily shot down. One of the former was killed by Captain Lacy, who placed it *hors de combat* at the first shot. Shortly afterwards, another tiger was routed out of a bamboo brake; but this, though wounded by several shots, rushed at the beaters, who gave way, and it escaped.

The game in this tract had now been thoroughly alarmed, and we were obliged to change our ground, proceeding to a patch of jungle about five miles distant, which must have covered five or six hundred acres. This patch was completely surrounded by the beaters, placed at intervals, like skirmishers but farther apart, who closed in towards the point where the elephants were stationed. Some small beasts of prey soon made their appearance, and great numbers of snakes, of from thirteen or fourteen inches in length to four or five feet, which were destroyed by the servants on foot; but no deer were here started, a very good reason for suspecting the place was much frequented by leopards and tigers, which proved to be the case, for three large tigers made their appearance simultaneously. One was riddled with bullets, but the other two escaped, the beaters being very timid. If they had raised a loud shout, and rushed upon the beasts in a body, they would probably have frightened them into running past the elephants, and we should have had an opportunity of peppering them.

The beaters had now contracted their line into a very narrow semi-circle, and but a small portion of the jungle remained unsearched;

but there were indications, such as the shaking of the grass and bushes, that some large beast was here concealed, and the cries of the men apprised us that it was a tiger. The beast was very unwilling, however, to leave the cover, and the beaters disregarded all our shouts and signs to them to close in. I was of opinion that the elephants should be advanced upon the tiger, and not being able to make my driver understand what I wanted, I sang out to Captain Lacy (with whom was Angbang, the interpreter), but he was afraid this would induce the beast to rush at the beaters, who would be sure to give way, and let it escape. He, however, directed one of the elephants to move round to the rear, and endeavour to induce it to come forward. This movement was successful, and the tiger made a sudden rush and sprung up at the Rajah's howdah, to which it clung with its claws, and would undoubtedly have speedily seized one of the occupants had they not saluted it with a steady volley, which sent it down under the elephant's stomach.

Judging from my own experience, I believe the tiger is in general a somewhat cowardly animal. When attacked by a hunter, it will, if possible, try to escape. Tigers that have once preyed upon man, I am firmly convinced, retain their liking for human flesh, and become confirmed man-eaters. These man-eaters frequently display the most audacious courage, even entering large and populous villages in search of a victim; but the only other cases in which I have known tigers show a bold front is when they are mortally wounded. Then they are perfect devils, whose sole object seems to be to have as dear a revenge as possible. Their eyes glare, and appear to be starting from their head; their lips are drawn up, showing their terrible fangs to perfection; and their hoarse roar of defiance is something appalling. At the sound of it a native will bolt up the nearest tree like a mad monkey, and his black features will become the colour of muddy cream.

The scene on the present occasion, but for the danger, would have been ludicrous. When the tiger began to roar, and its determination to fight became evident, the beaters and foot attendants disappeared with magical rapidity. Some few climbed into the thorn bushes: where the others got to I could not say for the life of me.

For a single second the tiger seemed stunned by the smart fire with which he had been received; but the moment he regained his feet, he came full tilt at my elephant. His white breast was crimson with blood, and blood was dropping from his mouth. He was desperately wounded, but had still sufficient life and strength to make himself a formidable adversary. Leaning over the side of my howdah, I fired all four barrels of my rifle, but without effect; and the creature springing up with frightful fury, fixed itself on the neck of the elephant, and attacked the driver. The poor wretch yelled in his fright, and fell to the ground, followed by the enraged brute, who would soon have made short work of him had not the sagacious elephant interfered. Seizing the monster round the neck with its trunk, it swung it up above my head and brought it to the earth with a tremendous crash. It did not move again; but the elephant, trumpeting angrily, dashed upon it with fury, impaled it with its tusks, threw it many times into the air, and trampled it under foot. I was afraid the enraged creature would shake the howdah from its back, for I had no control of it; but one of the native chiefs who was with me got upon its neck, and succeeded in pacifying it.

The tiger's claws had caught the driver's thigh, and ploughed up the flesh from the hip to the knee. He was not, however, dangerously hurt. The elephant's neck was also slightly torn.

In the mangled carcass of the tiger we found eleven bullet-holes, a sufficient proof of the tenacity of life in the cat tribe. This was the best day's sport in which I have taken a part. Our bag consisted of three tigers, two leopards, twenty-seven deer and antelopes, one hyæna and two lynxes; besides several animals which were wounded and got away, doubtless to die.

Leaving the beaters and servants, of whom only about a dozen were visible, to collect themselves and return at their leisure, we rode back to Tatsong, which we reached about seven o'clock in the evening.

CHAPTER VIII.

Dinner at the Rajah's palace.—His Highness elated.—Elephant stables.—White elephant.—Trade of the country.—Productions.—Elephant hunting.—Christmas Day.—An elephant hunt.—Its failure.—A second expedition.—Exciting adventure with a large male elephant.—Terror of the herd.—Cruelty of the Rajah.—Affecting tenderness of an elephant dam for its calf.—Long march of the beaters and servants.—A day's rest.—The Rajah offended.—Leave Tatsong.—Three villages seen.—People at work.—Four large brooks.—Snipe.—Very large bag made.

DEC. 24.—We dined at the palace last night after our return from the hunting expedition. Our own servants cooked for us and attended us during dinner, which was laid out on mats on the floor in a large hall on the second story of the palace. The Rajah ate his meal alone in an adjoining compartment, and the native attendants and officers also dined apart. They appeared to eat no flesh, and their food consisted of fruits, vegetables and boiled rice. I know, however, that the natives of this part do partake of flesh occasionally; though rice and vegetables form the chief part of their diet.

Large quantities of palm toddy were consumed, and I am sorry to say that before we took our leave, his Highness was in a merry condition. He was highly delighted with the day's sport, and spoke of making a second expedition. He informed us that the destruction of life in his territory by tigers was very great, and they seldom destroyed many either by poison, pitfalls, or hunting them. Some years ago, four persons were seized by tigers in one day in the neighbourhood of Tatsong.

Taking advantage of an invitation given to us by the Rajah last evening, we went this afternoon to look over his elephant stables. The Rajah himself conducted us, and was evidently greatly pleased with the praise we bestowed upon his beasts. He possessed sixty-three ordinary elephants of various sizes, and two white ones, which he took care to inform us were sacred, and not to be touched by the hands of any save the priests who attended to them. Their colour was not white, but a kind of muddy drab; and they were much smaller than the common elephants. Round each of their fore legs they had a massive ring of gold set with precious stones, and huge gold ear-rings were also attached to their ears. They were not chained up, and had the run of the large shed where they were confined. One priest was constantly in attendance upon them; and twice a day they were taken out for exercise and to bathe.

The Rajah had no horses, and assured us that he should not care to use them if he had; as he preferred riding upon elephant-back, and thought it the safest method of travelling. He admired our horses, however, and said they were very graceful-looking animals.

In reply to our questions about the trade carried on by his subjects with the inhabitants of other parts of the country, the Rajah said that it was considerable, and consisted principally of ivory, wax, honey, pepper, betel-nuts, and gold dust; but they also took linen goods to Bangkok, together with bamboo poles, canes, cocoa-nuts, sandal-wood, lead and copper in small quantities, game and birds' feathers (particularly those of a species of jay and the pea-fowl), for exportation to China, &c., palm-oil, yams, figs, gutta-percha, and a few diamonds and rubies.

The pepper, figs, &c., were grown wild and not cultivated; and the gold dust was found in the beds of the streams emptying themselves into the Menam. I was informed that the diamonds and rubies were found in some low hill ranges between twenty and thirty miles (as nearly as I could judge by what the Rajah said) from Tatsong, and that the copper and lead was procured from quarries in the same neighbourhood; but no regular mines were worked. I also learned from the Rajah, through our interpreter, that a large number of the inhabitants of Tatsong are professional elephant hunters, and they kill the animal in a great variety of ways. Sometimes they dig pitfalls, but this method is not much esteemed, as without great cunning is exercised in covering the holes, the sagacity of the elephant warns him of the danger. Occasionally a large party of natives surround an elephant and spear him to death; but the favourite method of killing them is by shooting them with firearms. The guns and muskets used are mostly of European make; but they have also pieces manufactured in Burmah and in China. These huntsmen also capture the wild elephants, and break them in for general use. They are captured in the same manner as that in vogue in India.

DEC. 25.—Christmas Day, but no plum-pudding and delicious underdone roast beef. However, we fared very well off a nice haunch of venison, and specially indulged in a bottle of sherry in honour of the occasion. In the evening the Rajah paid us a visit, and we shot pigeons and pea-fowl in the forest together. We bagged, between the four guns, fifty-two pigeons, eighteen pea-fowl, a stork, and six pheasants. The Rajah is a good shot, but the birds are wild, and, owing to their keeping in the tops of the tallest trees, difficult to shoot. We have arranged for an elephant hunt to-morrow.

DEC. 26.—The Rajah overslept himself, and when we presented ourselves at the palace about half-past four a.m., we were delayed an hour before his Highness was ready.

A large party of the native elephant hunters were in attendance, to conduct us to the best ground and find the game. We were mounted on our horses, intending to ride to the scene of action; but the Rajah, who was on elephant-back, insisted that we should come into his howdah, and we complied, sending our horses back to camp.

For three hours we were passing through an unbroken but not very dense forest before a herd of elephants was discovered. We immediately left the howdah, and proceeded with the hunters to cautiously approach them. These men displayed great timidity, and instead of going close up to the elephants before firing, they commenced to fire when quite a hundred yards off. This was almost useless, as the distance was too great for the bullets to take much effect, and the animals were alarmed before we could get near enough to have an effective shot. Nevertheless, three elephants fell, the huntsmen, sixty or seventy in number, having expended seven or eight rounds of ammunition per man to effect this slaughter, which ought not to have cost more than a score of well-directed shots.

The Rajah became very angry with the hunters for firing in this manner, as it deprived himself and us of a fair shot, and ordered that they should not fire at all when the next herd should be met with; but no more elephants could be found, and we returned disappointed to Tatsong. It was arranged, however, that the following day we should again try our luck.

Dec. 27.—We started this morning before daybreak, taking with us only nine of the native hunters, to serve as guides to finding the game. We had small success during the early part of the day, the only animal seen and shot being an antelope. The ground traversed was near that shot over yesterday, which in our opinion was not a very wise arrangement; but of course we did not like to appear dissatisfied, and therefore did not give expression to our opinion.

After a long, wearisome ramble, interrupted by several halts for refreshment, we turned towards home about four o'clock in the afternoon, having been out twelve hours. Between five and six o'clock, we came suddenly upon a small herd of fifteen elephants. The large male, their leader, was an exceedingly fine animal, standing at least ten or eleven feet high. Several others were scarcely inferior to him in size: indeed, the whole herd was of animals of above the average bulk. Three of them were calves—one quite a little thing, not more than a few months old. When we first discovered them it was sucking, being so small that it could hardly reach the dam's udder.

We came upon them so unexpectedly, that before we could get our rifles ready the opportunity for a good shot was lost. Our own elephant halted the instant he saw his wild companions, and they, after staring at him suspiciously for a moment or two, began to move away, though slowly, as if they were not quite satisfied whether there was danger in the wind or not. By the time our driver had commanded the sagacious brute to kneel down, and we had descended from the howdah, the herd was three hundred yards off; but they had stopped, and were bending down the boughs of the trees with their trunks, so that the young ones could get at the tender shoots and leaves.

Commanding the servants to keep back, ourselves and the Rajah advanced slowly towards them, always keeping a tree or thick bush in front of us to hide our approach. But notwithstanding all our caution they seemed to be aware of our manœuvring, and when we got to within a hundred yards of them commenced to move away again. At a little distance they halted once more, and remained quietly feeding upon the leaves of the trees until we again got to within about a hundred yards of them, when they moved off a little faster than before. This tantalising work continued for nearly half an hour, during which time we could never get nearer than from a hundred to a hundred and fifty yards, which, powerful as our breech-loading rifles were, was too great a distance for an effective fire.

At length we thought of trying to surround them, and approach from different sides, the understanding being that none of us should fire until we were apprised of the position of our companions. This was to prevent accidents from random shots. Our interpreter having been left with the other servants, we could not make the Rajah understand this arrangement, and so I took him with me.

Our plan was successful. The elephants first discovered the advance of Captain Lacy in front of them, and immediately commenced to move right down upon the spot where myself and the Rajah were crouching behind a large tree trunk. The first shot came from Mr. Grant on the right, and we promptly followed up his attack with three shots directed against the leading male. This drove the whole herd towards Captain Lacy, who received them with five shots, fired in rapid succession. The terrified animals, finding themselves surrounded on all sides, crowded together right in front of us, screaming and trumpeting in a pitiful manner, with their trunks elevated straight in the air.

Our breech-loading rifles enabled us to fire

very rapidly; and in a few minutes the big male and two others were on the ground. The herd, now terrified to the verge of madness, made a sudden rush and broke away; but as they passed the Rajah cruelly fired at the little calf and brought it down. I shall never forget the scene that followed. The dam rushed about franticly, making the ground tremble with her great weight; and in her wild excitement tearing down great branches from the trees. Her screaming was dreadful, and the caresses she bestowed upon the dying calf (for it was not killed outright) heart-rending. Suddenly she seemed to remember from whence the fatal shot had proceeded, and made a desperate charge towards us. It was well for the Rajah and myself that the firing of Mr. Grant and Captain Lacy diverted her attention. One bullet struck her tusk and broke it off about six inches from the root.

I was almost as much horrified as if I had witnessed the murder of a human being; and had not our lives been in actual danger I would not have lifted my rifle against her. Three or four more shots brought her to the earth; but even in her death agony she stretched her trunk towards the body of her now dead calf. From this time I could not help holding the Rajah in contempt in my own mind; for even the excitement of the moment can not be pleaded in excuse for the wanton slaughter of an animal so young that it was quite useless when killed.

This incident led me to think deeply upon the slaughter of wild animals, and of elephants in particular. The elephant is such an intelligent and gentle beast, and so useful to man, that its destruction, even for the sake of its ivory tusks, can scarcely be justified. It is true it does much damage to the crops of the natives; but it is, otherwise, in its wild state a perfectly harmless creature, never attacking man until injured, and but very seldom then. However illogical my reasoning may have been, it led me to determine that I would not again take part in an elephant hunt.

It was eight o'clock in the evening before we reached Tatsong. We were quite tired out, and during the day the servants, who accompanied us on foot, must have tramped forty miles at the least; but they are a hardy and enduring race of men. I have forgotten to say that besides the tusks of the elephants they have brought away a large quantity of the flesh for eating, especially that of the calf. The parts they appear to prefer are the feet, trunks, and tongues; but many broad steaks are also cut from the back.

DEC. 28. — A day devoted entirely to rest. In the evening we shot pea-fowl and pheasants, and also met with the wild jungle fowl. Areca trees are very abundant in the forest. The Rajah did not make his appearance to-day.

DEC. 29. — As it is our intention to leave Tatsong to-morrow, we went this evening to bid the Rajah farewell. We had seen nothing of him since the elephant hunt; and whether or no I had made my disgust at his conduct on that occasion too manifest, or whether he had, with the capriciousness of an Eastern ruler, taken offence at something else, it is impossible to say ; but he refused to see us. A circumstance that caused us a great deal of uneasiness at the time, and not a little surprise, as he had seemed to all of us a man of kind and amiable disposition.

It occurred to us that if his Highness should take it into his head to throw any obstacle in the way of the further prolongation of our journey, we should be in an awkward pickle, as we could not dare advance in open defiance of him. This thought hastened our departure, and at three o'clock the next morning we left Tatsong, making a wide circle round the village to avoid disturbing the inhabitants. By eight o'clock we calculated we had advanced twelve miles, and we halted for a couple of hours' rest. Resuming our journey, we did not get along quite so well, on account of the increased density of the forest, and the luxuriant undergrowth; but we extended our day's march to about twenty miles before we lay to for the night. Our custom now was to keep pace with the oxen and attendants, and not permit them to push forward or lag behind. We found this the most expedient and safest plan; as, though the servants were trustworthy men, and careful, they were scarcely fit to encounter any sudden emergency that might occur, such as an attack from ill-disposed natives, or a chance dispute: for these blacks are, as a rule, quarrelsome with men of their own colour, but of a different nationality. During our stay at Tatsong several trifling disputes arose between our men and the inhabitants, which were only prevented from breaking out into a serious disturbance by our removing our camp out of the town, and forbidding the servants to enter the place.

DEC. 31.—We saw three villages in the course of the day, but did not pass through any of them, though we met many of the people on the roads and at work in the forest, the latter picking fruit and collecting the wild honey which is very abundant. None of them evinced much astonishment at the sight of our cavalcade; but some with whom we communicated were very inquisitive, demanding where we were going, what we wanted there, &c. With the exception of a few insignificant patches of rice, there was no grain, or vegetables of any kind, under cultivation near these villages; neither were any domestic animals seen, not even dogs. There were no pagodas in or near these hamlets.

We were now shaping our course diagonally in the direction of the Menam, the banks of which we were anxious to reach again if the ground was practicable. During the day's march of nine miles we crossed four large brooks, one with eight feet of water in its bed, except at the fordable spots. About these brooks we shot a great number of snipe, of a kind twice the size of those found in England. In the trees about here, too, there were immense numbers of storks' nests; and though we could find no four-footed game, I have never seen any country better supplied with birds of all kinds. After the tent was pitched we made the following handsome little bag: viz., eighty-nine snipe, three pea-fowl, three storks (many more of these birds could have been easily obtained), fifteen partridges, and one bird, apparently of the starling tribe, but which had not been met with previously.

CHAPTER IX.

Regain banks of the Menam.—Rate of progress.—Gigantic forests.—Height of the trees.—Appearance of the river.—Flamingoes.—Frilled lizards.—Marshy ground.—Alligators and tigers.—Disturbed by the noise of wild beasts.—Fight between a bull-buffalo and a rhinoceros.—Extraordinary display of fire-flies.—Tigers and buffalo.—Cross a tributary of the Menam.—Flying squirrels.—Dangerous marshy ground.—Loss of an ox, and narrow escape of Mr. Grant.—Miserable plight.—Another ox lost.—Desperate position.—Apathy of our servants.—Strange appearance of the trees.—Illness of Mr. Grant.—He and a servant attacked by fever.—Weed of which cattle are fond.—Continued illness of Mr. Grant.

JANUARY 1, 1870.—The first day of the new year and consequently a noteworthy one, even in the deep solitude of a Siam forest. We were marching, with intervals to rest the oxen, all day, being anxious to reach the Menam as soon as possible. We arrived on its banks about half-past five o'clock in the afternoon, having made seventeen miles — a good long stretch considering we had marched twenty miles the day before yesterday. These distances would not be great for a man to perform; but, as I have frequently remarked before, the oxen plod along at a very slow pace. They are consequently a long time on the road, and an average of six hours' journeying a day (which means from twelve to sixteen miles, according to the character of the country) is all that can be expected of them.

I give no particular description of the country from the simple fact that two words will give the reader nearly all the information that he can possibly have. Those two words are—gigantic forest. No country in the world can equal this country for forests; and no country save New Guinea has more gigantic trees. Hence, though the appearance of the landscape is grand as well as beautiful, there must of necessity be a certain sameness in a written description of it; because there is so little to describe but forest scenery. Some of the trees here were, I am sure, two hundred and fifty feet in height; in fact the monkeys who inhabit the topmost branches look quite dwarfed, and the parrots and other birds appear like mere specks; and they are far out of reach of shot. Even with wire cartridge we could not hit them strongly enough to kill them, except in a few odd instances.

The river here presents a magnificent body of water to view. It is about three quarters of a mile wide, and the opposite bank appears as thickly clothed with forest as that on which we stand. The trees overhang the water for a distance of fifty or sixty yards, and there are large beds of tall reeds growing in the shallow water, which are a favourite resort of numbers of splendid rose-coloured flamingoes. In a swampy marsh we found some curious nests of this bird. They were constructed of mud in the shape of a pyramid about three feet high, but hollowed out at the top to receive the eggs. The bird sits on its nest with its legs hanging down, something like those of a man on horseback. The only nest that we could get close to contained four muddy-white eggs, about the size of those of the swan, or a little smaller.

This marsh was also remarkable for the myriads of frilled lizards which harboured in it. These little reptiles were three or four inches in length, and had round the neck a membrane or frill like a bat's wing, which completely hid their heads from view. When, however, they were not disturbed, the frill lay flat over the back; giving them the appearance of having a very loose skin.

JAN. 2.—Thick forest and tracts of marshy land compelled us to advance in a zig-zag, and we were frequently out of sight of the river, which varied in breadth from about twelve to fourteen hundred yards. Several times when near its bank we saw an odd alligator or two; but these reptiles are not numerous in any part of the country we have visited. Tigers, however, are here as numerous as in any district we have passed through. No fewer than five were seen in the course of the day and evening. One gentleman received a bullet behind his shoulder, which put an end to his troubles and pleasures. The others beat a retreat the instant they were disturbed; one of them being badly hurt at long range, and probably only got away to die.

In the mud near the water we saw innumerable prints of buffalo hoofs, and places where these animals had been wallowing in the mud. There were also traces of deer, seemingly of several different species.

After our tent was pitched, we shot, as usual, in the forest round about. To-night we pushed along the edge of the water, and knocked over some beautiful little ducks. They were white and grey in colour, but splendidly variegated about the head, neck, wings and tail with red, blue, and green. Other birds seen were flamingoes, storks, herons, ibises, snipes, bitterns, pigeons, quails, hawks, crows, parrots, and finches in great variety.

During the night we were greatly disturbed by the wild animals, which came down to the river to drink and bathe. The moon was about full, and the light it gave so brilliant that we could distinctly see elephants, rhinoceroses, buffalo,* and other animals sporting in the water. There were many hundreds of the various species, and it was rather dangerous work to approach so large a number; but we went, and were rewarded with a fine buffalo and a couple of small antelopes. Each species

---

* These buffalo, which are only found in the wildest parts of the country, appear to be the descendants of some which have escaped from captivity, and gradually become wild.

kept to itself in the water, but they were very close together, and we witnessed a fight between a bull buffalo and a rhinoceros, in which, however, neither seemed to be much hurt.

The trees here are covered with the magnificent fire-flies described previously. The sight is grand in the extreme, and has almost a supernatural appearance. It is difficult to conceive that the brilliant sparks, appearing and disappearing with such uniform regularity, proceed from insects ; and any one seeing this extraordinary display for the first time, and not being aware of the cause of it, would certainly say that the forest was illuminated with hundreds of thousands of tiny lamps. We have seen a few of these flies every night lately ; but it is only occasionally, and in the immediate neighbourhood of the river, that they show themselves in such immense numbers.

The cries of tigers and other beasts of prey echoed through the forests all night, and between one or two o'clock in the morning, the loud bellowing of a buffalo announced that it had been so unfortunate as to fall into the clutches of one of the striped monarchs of the wilderness. It is said that the tiger dare not attack a herd of buffaloes, and that the bull buffalo is a match for a full-grown tiger. I cannot confirm this; but I do know that buffaloes are frequently pulled down by tigers, and I have seen the partly-consumed carcasses lying in the vicinity of a tiger's haunt.

JAN. 3.—This morning we crossed a large river running from the north-east, and emptying itself into the Menam. We proceeded three or four miles up its right bank, and finding that there was no chance of being able to ford across it, we constructed rafts for the goods, and swam the horses and cattle over. It took us three hours and a half to cross, including time spent in felling young trees, &c., for constructing the rafts. The width of the river was, perhaps, three hundred yards. Like the Menam, both of its banks were covered with dense forest. In the trees about this river we saw, beside numerous monkeys, some small flying animal—a flying squirrel, flying fox, lemur, or some animal of that class. It was very quick in its movements, and all our endeavours to shoot one for a closer examination were unsuccessful. They kept at a great height from the ground, and it was our opinion that their fur offered resistance to the shot, as several times we felt sure they had been struck.

We found ourselves in a regular fix on the opposite shore, on account of the boggy nature of the ground. The oxen sank in to the knees; the horses were in an even worse plight, and were unable to carry our weight through the tenacious mud. We were compelled to dismount, and for the next four hours we had a terrible struggle. In that space of time we did not get over more than a mile of this accursed bog, and two of the oxen stuck fast and could not be extricated. To save the poor brutes from a lingering death they were shot. Mr. Grant had also a narrow escape; for pushing forward adventurously to find the best ground, he slipped into a mud-hole, and was buried to his arm-pits. It took us half an hour to dig him out; and he was then pretty well exhausted. Two or three of the men afterwards met with the same accident; but they were rescued with less difficulty.

At length we became so exhausted that we were almost ready to give up, and lie down to die. Fortunately, and as if directed by the special hand of Providence, we found a small patch of firmer ground, not more than half an acre in extent. Here we contrived to pitch our tent, and make arrangements for passing the night; but we could not find any dry fuel with which to make a fire. This caused us some suffering, as we were wet through, covered with mud, and badly in need of a hot meal. The cattle also suffered much from need of forage.

A night of misery and a gloomy daybreak. Mud beneath, and thick foliage above that nearly shuts out the light of heaven; for this morass is covered with a forest growth which proves that the mud is not of any great depth. There is not much comfort to be gleaned from that fact, however, since it is evidently deep enough to make it a matter of doubt whether we shall ever get out of this place alive.

At daybreak we held a consultation as to the course to be pursued. At first we thought of beating a retreat; but that mile of mud that had taken four hours to conquer, could not be got through again in the present weak state of ourselves and the cattle. Besides, we had found one tolerably firm piece of ground, and we hoped it might be the forerunner of others. It was reasonable to expect that the farther inland from the river we could get, the better we might expect the ground to be. At all events, we must take our chance; and to advance seemed to us less dangerous than to attempt a retreat.

Our servants were quite lethargic with fear and exhaustion, and we had some difficulty in arousing them to action. Akbar Nanee was the most self-possessed, and encouraged by the example of this man and our own assumed cheerfulness, they made an exertion to get our little caravan under weigh. As we had expected, we found small oases of firm ground at frequent intervals; but the bog between them was frightful. In eight hours we travelled something less than five miles, at a rough calculation; and another ox had to be destroyed. It became fixed in the mud, and in trying to drag it out with ropes, its leg was pulled out of the socket. In consequence of this loss of our cattle, a good part of the most unnecessary articles in our baggage was abandoned.

Our attendants have now entirely lost their pluck. Two men sat down with the intention of quietly perishing without making any further exertion to save their lives; and it was not until we had resorted to violence that they would continue to perform their duties. They did not, however, show anything of a mutinous spirit; but with the apathy of their race wished to be suffered to lie down and die in peace.

We had, fortunately, a good supply of brandy and other stimulants with us, and were thus enabled to hold out hours after we should otherwise have succumbed. When night began to draw on, we were undoubtedly nearing a more comfortable tract of country; and though we were obliged to halt, we were considerably cheered by being able to light fires and procure some coarse grass for the oxen and horses. During this night the trees were so thickly crowded wth fire-flies that they looked like masses of phosphorescent light.

JAN. 5.—Owing to our wearied condition we did not start from our camping-place till mid-day. We had now no more than about six inches of sticky mud, but it was of a slimy, slippery consistence, and the oxen and horses fell frequently. We could not yet ride the latter, and the poor beasts had scarcely sufficient strength left to bear the baggage.

The trees here were tall, with trunks of immense size. There was no undergrowth at all, and but very little coarse grass growing in patches here and there. No monkeys or other animals were to be seen, and scarcely a bird. The silence was death-like, and the solitude frightful. I am not surprised that the blacks were quite disheartened.

We got along very well considering the

exhausted condition of men and cattle, and the wretched character of the ground. Halts, of course, were frequent, and the total length of the day's journey did not exceed eight miles; but we were then on tolerably firm footing, and had found some low bushes, the tender shoots of which were very acceptable to the beasts. This spot was overrun with the small frilled lizard, spoken of on a former occasion as inhabiting marshy land. No animals or birds seen, and no sounds heard save the melancholy sighing of the breeze through the tree-tops.

JAN. 6.—Nothing particular to retard our journeying to-day except weakness. We want to lie by for a rest; but the country is hardly favourable for that yet. Our feet have become thoroughly sodden, and covered with sores, especially those of the blacks, who do not wear shoes but a kind of sandal. We are living entirely upon biscuit, bread, and potted meat. There is no lack of water, for pools of it are found at every hundred yards or so. We are mostly distressed by want of grass for the cattle, and are obliged to cut down branches from the trees in order that they may eat the leaves. We are marching in a south-east direction, supposing the Menam to be but a mile or two distant on our right hand. Day's march, about eight miles, through forest. Country improving rapidly. Good grass at halting-point, though in small patches.

JAN. 7.—To our great joy we reached the boundary of the morass about ten o'clock this morning. The country beyond is covered with the never terminating forest; but there is undergrowth, which, though troublesome, affords good food for horses and oxen. Here we have determined to halt until our strength is thoroughly recruited.

JAN. 8.—Mr. Grant was very ill all day, suffering apparently from jungle fever. All of us, including the blacks, are more or less unwell. Myself and Lacy went out in search of game. We neither found any nor met with traces of its being in the neighbourhood. The only living creatures seen were some flying squirrels, birds, lizards, and a small green snake. We shot two snipes and cooked them for Grant, but he could not eat.

JAN. 9.—It being very desirable and necessary for the preservation of health that we should obtain a supply of fresh meat, and there being evidently no large game in this region, we broke up our camp this morning, and moved south-west, to get nearer the river, where we were pretty certain of finding deer and antelopes. We discovered that we were farther away from the Menam than we thought. We had marched twelve miles in a diagonal direction before we had reached it. We should have gone over a greater distance had not Mr. Grant been too ill to sit his horse and expressed a great desire for rest.

We found a very good spot under a banyan tree for pitching the tent, and having made our patient as comfortable as possible under the circumstances, we rode a few miles down the river, and had the good fortune to shoot a small antelope and a few ducks. Mr. Grant was able to partake of a little broth made from the venison; but during the night he was so bad that we felt quite alarmed on his account. He is in a high state of fever, and one of the native attendants is also laid up.

JAN. 10. — The cattle, which were much reduced by their late exertion, look better already. The attendants fed them with a weed which grows very abundantly just here in the Menam. It is found in all the streams and rivers throughout the country, growing under water, and cattle and buffalo are very fond of it. There is, moreover, plenty of good grass about here. No improvement in Mr. Grant's condition. The sick black has also evidently got an attack of fever; but we cannot get the stupid fellow to take the quinine which we offer to him.

During the 11th, 12th, 13th, and 14th, there was no perceptible change in Mr. Grant. On the latter day he seemed much worse, and we gave up all hope of his recovery. The other man, notwithstanding his obstinate refusal to take any remedies, got better, and does not appear the worse for his sickness.

During those days we shot over the ground near our tent, and bagged a fine pea-fowl, partridges, ducks, snipe, &c., and a couple of antelopes. At night buffalo and deer came down to the river to drink, and also a rhinoceros or two. We shot one buffalo.

CHAPTER X.

Improvement in Mr. Grant's condition.—Beautiful little finch.—Resume our journey.—Small plains.—Sharp encounter with a rhinoceros.—A rhinoceros killed with a single shot.—Boats and rafts pass down the river.—Reeds, mosquitos, and gnats.—Extraordinary appearance of the clouds.—The forest appears to be a mass of silvery light.—Description of the country.—Find remains of a buffalo.—A tiger shot.—Dense forest.—Compelled to camp out.—Men sent in search of us.

JAN. 15.—We were greatly rejoiced to-day at a decided improvement in Mr. Grant's state. He is far less feverish, and has a ravenous appetite; he would have eaten much more than we thought it prudent to permit him.

While in the forest to-day, I shot a beautiful little finch. The crown of its head, back of the neck, and shoulders were sky-blue. The upper part of the body and wings were nearly black, the tail and wings being marked with crimson; and the throat and breast were crimson, gradually fading into a pinky-white on the belly. In size it was rather less than a sparrow.

The roaring of a tiger was heard during the night, and the trees were again splendidly illuminated by the fire-flies. Nothing material occurred in the course of the next three days. Mr. Grant made rapid strides towards recovery, and amused himself with stuffing the small birds which we shot for his collection. Since we have been in the country he has got together nearly a hundred different species, several of which he considers are quite new to science, and others but imperfectly known and described.

Myself and Lacy passed the time, which hung heavily on our hands, in shooting and wandering about the forest. We made several excursions in search of a tiger, but were unsuccessful, though we had often heard the cry of the animal during the past week.

JAN. 16.—Mr. Grant being well enough to endure the exertion of riding, we broke up our camp, and proceeded on our way south, keeping along the bank of the river, which was here about three quarters of a mile wide. Many small streams ran into it, some of which were nearly choked up with reeds. The country here seems more fertile than farther north ; and we were pleased to again meet with troops of monkeys, for it is a singular fact that wherever these animals are found there is generally an abundance of large game and birds. Parrots are as plentiful as in any of the forests hitherto passed through.

The ground eastward seems to rise in low undulating hills, but they are of insignificant elevation, and not arranged in chains or ranges. The forest, though dense, is not unbroken, and we passed over several plains almost destitute of trees; but these were of such small extent as to scarcely justify particular mention. The whole face of the country may be called one vast forest of gigantic trees.

JAN. 17.—While crossing one of the small plains, or glades, such as were described yesterday, we met with a large single-horned rhinoceros. He was standing, when first seen, perfectly motionless — perhaps listening, for they are very quick of ear, and some sound from our party must have reached him. Halting the men, myself and Lacy dismounted and cautiously neared the brute, which beyond a slight movement of the head gave no sign of life; and looked uncommonly like a huge model of a rhinoceros, such as I have seen in some museum.

I would here remark that we always attacked the dangerous game on foot for these reasons: that it is impossible to take a steady aim from horseback; and, moreover, it is necessary to approach so close for an effective shot, that in the event of the beast making a sudden rush, he is nearly sure to be upon you before you can spur your horse out of the way; besides, it is ten to one that the latter does not become frightened and unmanageable. It would be madness to attack a tiger on horseback, and nearly as dangerous to repeat the experiment with a rhinoceros.

The sight of the rhinoceros is very dim, and owing to this circumstance if you are careful not to make any noise, you may get quite close to it without being observed. There were trees within forty yards of our rhinoceros, so that we were well concealed; but there being some bushes still nearer to it, we crawled forward under their shelter, and gave it the first shot behind the shoulder from a distance of only twenty yards. Up to this moment the beast had remained perfectly quiet; but on receipt of the bullet he wheeled round and charged with the rapidity of a flash of lightning before Captain Lacy had time to fire a shot. I had not time to rise and get out of the way, and only saved myself by rolling over and over in a very undignified manner. It is almost marvellous that the rhinoceros did not see me; but his whole attention was concentrated on the bush, which he appeared to think was the foe from whence the attack proceeded. He trampled over it, breaking it down with the weight of his huge body, and commenced to rip it to pieces with his horn.

Meantime Captain Lacy blazed away with both barrels from behind a tree trunk, and though the beast was badly hurt it charged at him desperately, which gave me an opportunity of recovering my rifle, which was lying near the bush. It was difficult now to hit the rhinoceros in a vital part, for it was tearing about wildly amongst the bushes, evidently in search of its foe. We discharged eight or nine shots at it before it fell, and every time we fired it charged furiously in the direction of the report of the rifle, and it required some nimbleness to get out of its way. Even when it sank to the ground it made strenuous efforts to rise again, and received six more bullets before it was finished off. At this juncture Mr. Grant came up with two spare rifles, alarmed at the continued firing and great commotion which he had witnessed from the distance.

Our aiming in this little affair had been very bad, for though no less than nineteen bullets had penetrated this beast, not one of them had hit a really vital part; and it had been literally bled to death by the number of its wounds. In curious contrast with this difficulty in slaying a rhinoceros was another adventure that happened that same evening while myself and Lacy were out searching for game after the tent had been pitched.

We had taken a rather long ramble, and darkness was coming on fast, so that we struck the river and began to hasten back to our camp, distant a good three miles. Not half a mile of this distance was got over when we came upon a very large rhinoceros standing in the water about twenty yards from the bank. We were so anxious to get back to our tent before darkness had set in that we should probably have passed the brute without interfering with it had it not come out of the water and made a demonstration of disputing our passage. Captain Lacy dropped upon his knee and fired, and the rhinoceros fell with a heavy shock. The muscular twitching of its limbs, which ceased in a minute or two, showed that it had been killed outright; and upon walking up to it we found that the bullet had actually penetrated the brain through the eye, which was more the effect of chance than design.

Besides rhinoceroses we have found the footprints of deer, wild elephants, boar, and buffalo in the soft earth and mud of the river bank; and all sorts of birds are very abundant. Mr. Grant informed us that during our absence a flock of some hundreds of flamingoes were feeding for more than an hour in the river abreast of our camp. He saw them repeatedly catch and swallow fish of considerable size.

Jan. 18.—We passed the carcass of the rhinoceros killed last night. Some beasts of prey have already been at it, and have torn away the flesh from the side lying uppermost, so that we can look into the cavity of the stomach. A flock of greedy buzzards flew away from it as we drew near, and, pitching upon the trees and bushes near at hand, only awaited our departure to recommence operations.

About half-past eight a long string of flat-bottomed boats and rafts passed us, going down the river with merchandise. They were propelled with long poles by the boatmen, who seemed greatly astonished when we hailed them; but they disregarded our request that they would stop and land. Their progress was much faster than ours, and in a very short time they had rounded a bend in the river and were out of sight.

In this part of the river there are immense quantities of tall reeds, which in some places prevented us from seeing the water. Millions of mosquitos and gnats harbour about these reeds, and are exceedingly tormenting, continually getting into our eyes and stinging every exposed part of our bodies without mercy. Here, also, there were great numbers of a large red fly with green wings, which attacked our cattle and horses and drove them half wild. It was in vain for us to go farther inland; wherever we went the flies followed us in clouds.

Eastward there are many low hills, covered like all other parts of the country with dense forest. By-the-by, the forest here is closely matted together with creepers, parasites, &c., a peculiarity not met with in all parts. Near the river the trees grow at wider intervals, and travelling is comparatively easy; but the forest is quite impenetrable. We did not march more than six miles to-day on account of the weakness of Mr. Grant. He has quite recovered from his attack of fever, but it has left him in a low and exhausted condition.

The clouds this evening presented an extraordinary yet beautiful appearance. Large masses of deep purple and light red clouds were arranged in such a manner as to produce the most curious and eccentric figures and shapes. We remarked that if any painter dared to represent such a strange mass of clouds, and with such abnormal tints and colours, his picture would excite more ridicule than any of the caricatures of *Punch*. People who never move from home can have but a poor idea of the wonders of nature as seen in eastern and tropical countries. In some parts of Siam we have met with a tree or shrub, the foliage of which is a brilliant crimson; but if any artist was to introduce such a tree into his landscape, would it not be thought that his imagination had been at work?

When darkness set in the forest became one mass of silvery light, so thickly were the fireflies clustering on the trees. The strangest sight, however, was on the opposite bank of the river, where the flies, owing to the distance, could not be distinctly seen, and yet the phosphorescent glitter of their lights was visible, making the trees appear exactly as if they were burning with a white flame. Many wild animals came down to the water, greatly disturbing our rest throughout the night. As the roar of the tiger resounded from many parts of the forest, we kept large fires burning as a protection to ourselves and the cattle.

JAN. 19.—Mr. Grant entreated that we would halt for a day, to give him an opportunity of obtaining rest, of which he was sadly in need. Lacy and myself, therefore, taking Akbar and two more of the attendants, went off for a day's sport. Quite close to our camp we found the fresh footmarks of a large tiger. It had actually been within eighty or a hundred yards of the spot where the oxen were picketed, and had, no doubt, only been deterred from attacking them by the large fires which we had kept burning brightly.

We decided to follow the track of this brute, and endeavour to destroy it; but after tracing it for nearly two miles, the beast had entered a tangled brake which we could not penetrate.

Working our way amidst the trees as well as we could, we made a north-east course, being constantly obliged to have recourse to the compass for guidance. After three hours' real hard work, we calculated we were not more than five or six miles from our camp, so slow had our progress been. These forests were full of peafowl and the three different species of monkeys mentioned and described on a former occasion; but though their cries and chattering proclaimed how numerous they were, the trees were so tall, and the masses of creeping plants that hung down so thick, that we seldom saw them; and to make use of our fire-arms was quite impossible, for we had scarcely elbow-room, and even had we shot a bird, it would not, in all probability, have reached the ground. Indeed, on the previous evening, we had tried to shoot pea-fowl in a similar maze to this, and of twelve birds at least that were killed, only two could be got at, and the servants had to climb the trees after those.

But to resume. In three hours we unexpectedly came to the outskirts of this forest track, and found the country beyond rather hilly, rough, and broken. The highest elevations, however, did not rise to a greater height than a hundred and fifty feet, or thereabouts. These hills were mostly covered with tall trees, at least two hundred feet in height; but there were here some patches of jungle growth so full of snakes and other reptiles that we could not enter them; and also some level plains clothed with bushes, where we surprised several small herds of buffalo, and shot three of them. We halted by the sides of the carcasses, lit a fire, and cooked some steaks that ate deliciously, no doubt partly because the tough work of the morning had made us ravenously hungry. After a short rest we despatched Akbar and the two servants back to the camp, with as much of the buffalo beef as they could carry; and made a fresh start ourselves, still pushing forward in a north-east direction.

Between one and two o'clock in the afternoon, we came upon the remains of a buffalo that had been pulled down by a tiger. The whole rear portion of the animal had been eaten away, and buzzards and small beasts of prey were busy upon what remained. Our advent, of course, put them to flight; but they did not retire very far, and remained on the outskirts of the forest, anxiously waiting until the coast should be clear. We had not, however, any intention of moving away; but knowing full well that the tiger would return to finish his meal, set about intrenching ourselves to give him a warm reception.

We had to wait a long while. It was nearly six o'clock in the evening before a warning growl sent the buzzards and lynxes flying, and our tiger, a magnificent animal more than six feet in length, stepped upon the scene. He commenced operations upon the remnants of the buffalo without loss of time, tearing away at them vigorously, quite unconscious of our presence and the fate that awaited him. Captain Lacy was the first to fire, aiming at the breast, which was full in front of us. The tiger dropped without a growl, falling flat on its belly, and lifting up its head gasped for breath. A shot from my rifle eased it of all pain; but it did not roll over when dead. It remained in a sitting posture, as though its meal had only been temporarily interrupted.

It was too late for us to think of skinning it. As it was, it was certain that it would be dark before we could possibly regain our camp; we therefore started off at once, leaving the tiger in the position in which it had died.

The thick forest tract was a source of great trouble to us, and we were frequently under the impression that we had lost our way. When it became dark—and unfortunately there was no moon—it was impossible for us to continue to read the compass, and down we sat, scarcely knowing what to do. We had not penetrated the forest very far as yet, and determined to try and make our way back to the spot where the buffalo had been shot. In this we were successful; for when we got clear of the trees there was sufficient starlight to guide us to the place. We found that the fire that had been lighted in the morning was still smouldering, and we speedily blew it up into a blaze, added more fuel, and cooked ourselves a good supper of buffalo beef: so that on the whole we did not fare so badly, especially as the night was warm, and we had taken the precaution to bring our cloaks with us.

At three o'clock in the morning it began to be daylight, and we started for our camp, advancing at the quickest pace possible, knowing that the anxiety of Mr. Grant at our prolonged absence would be very great. In spite of all our exertions, it was mid-day before we arrived at the tent, thoroughly beat. Mr. Grant was quite alarmed, feeling sure that some accident had befallen us, and had sent out all the attendants except one in search of us. We were rather surprised that we had not met with any of these men, who had gone out by twos, taking different directions. It was five o'clock in the afternoon before they had all returned; having, it is needless to say, been unsuccessful in their search.

This expedition had been so tiring that we found it advisable to lie by a second day; an arrangement that pleased Mr. Grant, who is afflicted with an unconquerable lassitude and desire to remain quiet.

CHAPTER XI.

Village in an unusually filthy state.—Inquisitiveness of the natives.—Fruit abundant.—Density of the population.—Large tracts cleared of timber.—Horrors of a night in a native hut.—Enormous number of rats.—Compelled to turn out.—Differences with our landlord.—Large river.—Slaughter of buffaloes.—Fauna met with.—Domestic animals.—Ferocious dog.—Tedious march.—Arrive at Siam.—Disposition of the natives.—Siamese dramatic entertainment.—Extensive rice fields.—Pretty scenery.—Arrival at Bangkok.—Meet with an Englishman, and are kindly entertained by him.—Floating houses.—Alteration of our arrangements.—Mr. Grant leaves for Rangoon.

JAN. 22.—The most important occurrence of this day's journey was the arriving at a village built on the banks of the Menam. It contained fifty-two huts and houses, some of them two stories in height; but there was no pagoda in or near it. The people were greatly astonished at our appearance, and seemed considerably more stupid and slothful in their habits than those we have communicated with previously. We did not feel at all encouraged to remain a night amongst them, partly on account of the filthy state of the place, and the horrid effluvia arising therefrom; and, accordingly, resumed our journey early in the afternoon and pushed on another eight miles, making about sixteen in all; in the course of which distance we have crossed five small and three large streams (all fordable) emptying themselves into the Menam.

Well watered as the country is, we can discover no signs of any part of it being under cultivation, though large tracts have been cleared of timber, much of which probably has been floated down to Bangkok. Some of the land is rather boggy, and in the rainy season is undoubtedly inundated. Two large alligators were seen in the river to-day, and one dead, lying in the mud on the bank.

Mr. Grant evidently requires a long period of rest to recover his strength. Every march that we take knocks him up, and to-night he is quite prostrate. We have decided to reach Bangkok — which we suppose to be distant about one hundred miles—as speedily as circumstances will permit.

JAN. 23.—Three hamlets passed through, and two others seen. The people betray much astonishment, and in one place, when they discovered that Angbang understood their language, made many inquiries about our business, &c., and particularly wanted to know where our horses were procured. A pagoda of small size was passed on the road between two of these villages; but, with the exception of one or two patches of rice, no cultivated ground. Fruit trees are abundant everywhere about here, growing wild; but I do not think they could possibly be improved by cultivation. However that may be, the fruit is far superior to that produced by European trees.

Round each village the ground has been cleared of timber; but we do not see a sign of any domestic creatures, save dogs, fowls, and pigs—in fact there are no others generally kept in any part of the country, except in the seaport towns.

JAN. 24.—As we advance we find the villages and hamlets appear in rapid succession. Some of these, too, are of considerable size, containing perhaps four or five hundred inhabitants. Fields of rice are also more frequently met with, and the people seem tolerably clean and orderly; though they scarcely come up to the standard of those farther north in this respect. Much timber has been felled, and one village that we passed was built almost entirely on rafts floating in the river. Other houses are built on piles. Wood is the principal material of which they are constructed. Several pagodas lay in our road, well-kept, fine-looking buildings, invariably sheltered with banyan trees and groves of palm. We saw monkeys here in the trees that grew close round the village, and hundreds of parrots perch upon the roofs of the houses; and in the villages which are built on the banks of the river, the storks have built many nests on the roofs.

We passed this night in a hamlet, and in order that Mr. Grant should have better accommodation than the tent afforded, we hired the use of an empty house. This house contained two stories, and a sort of garret in the roof above. The ground-floor appearing to be rather damp, we made our beds on the second, which was reached by a rough bamboo ladder. The night to us was a night of horrors on a small scale. Being wretchedly tired I fell asleep myself the moment I lay down; but I think a very few minutes could have elapsed before I was awakened by a sharp pain about the feet. I started up and the pain ceased. It was pitch dark, for there was only one small opening in the wall to admit air, and I could see nothing; but below there was a noise as of some one sprawling over the floor. I thought it was one of the men moving about (some of whom were sleeping below), and composed myself to rest again, to be again aroused by a pain about the feet and legs, as if something was gnawing them. There was also a noise as of a lot of dogs scampering about the room, and Mr. Grant sang out, and Lacy banged something upon the floor, and gave vent to an imprecation more forcible than elegant.

We had a lantern with us, and it was soon lighted, revealing a sight that might well have shocked the nerves of a weak person. Hundreds of rats were running about the room, and when disturbed by the light, bolted into holes in the walls and floor, and some of them actually ran up the wall in their efforts to escape, while five or six serpents hung by their tails from the bamboo ceiling, every now and then darting at a lizard, or such rats as came near them. My legs and feet were bitten and bleeding; Captain Lacy was in the same plight, and had also been bitten in the face, and Mr. Grant had a finger badly gnawed. Lacy killed several of the rats with his boot, and leaving the lantern alight, we hoped that we should not be further disturbed, and once more rolled ourselves in our blankets. Of the snakes we had no fear, knowing that they were harmless, and if left undisturbed would not come down from the ceiling.

It soon became evident that it was vain to hope for rest in this place. The rats speedily got used to the light, and came out of their holes in scores. We tried all sorts of means to prevent them from getting at us, but without success. Although we were uncomfortably warm, we wrapped our blankets tightly round us; but the tiresome vermin eat their way through to our feet and legs, parts that they particularly attacked. They also bit us about the face and neck, and at length came out in such swarms that we were compelled to vacate the place.

All this time a great noise had been going on below, and when we made our appearance we found that the men had fared as badly as ourselves. Two or three of them were severely bitten, and they had killed more than *two hundred* rats. The place was literally alive with them, and we were only too glad to get out to our tent.

JAN. 25.—Angbang found out that the house where we had passed part of last night had been abandoned on account of being overrun with vermin, and the owner had been guilty of an imposition in letting it to us; we therefore refused to pay him for its use. The fellow made a great noise, and collected a crowd of the inhabitants around us; but it was of no avail; he did not get his money.

We have now decidedly got into an inhabited and rudely cultivated district. Villages and small hamlets are numerous, and there are many patches of rice growing near the river, though not of any considerable extent. The land has been cleared to a great extent of forests, but there are still some large tracts, and much of the ground is covered with jungle and bamboo brakes, which, we are assured by the inhabitants, are much frequented by tigers. We, however, saw no traces of them or other large game, with the exception of a few antelope, several of which we shot.

JAN. 26.—Two hours' march brought us to a river of great size, six or seven hundred yards wide. Previous to this, we have found the country well watered with small streams and brooks, all running, of course, into the Menam. This river caused an impediment to our progress, as we did not dare attempt to cross it on rafts at this spot, where the current was rapid and strong. At the point where it joined the Menam, the latter river was quite a mile wide. Proceeding up its left bank for six miles, we came to a village called by the inhabitants Caganitroot, or, according to Captain Lacy's orthography, Cagannetroot. This was a large village, but straggling, and built amidst an uncleared forest district, so that it was not easy to ascertain its real extent. Many of the houses, as elsewhere, were built in the river on rafts. Plenty of boats were obtainable here, but they were so small as not to hold an ox with safety, and we were obliged to construct rafts for the conveyance of the cattle, hiring the boats to tow them across the river. These operations consumed the greater part of the 27th, and we did not move from the left bank until the morning of the 28th.

After marching five miles in a direct south direction we were compelled to alter our route to the east for some distance, in order to avoid an extensive tract of morass. This morass was destitute of trees, but it nourished thickets of thorn bushes, bearing a bright and pretty yellow flower. Three or four herds of buffalo were seen wallowing in the mud of the moister places, one of them numbering nearly a hundred beasts. We slaughtered four of them, and secured a good stock of the meat. The buffalo can generally be shot without much danger to the sportsman; but if the first bullet does not happen to mortally or badly wound it, it will sometimes attack him with great fierceness.

The country east of the morass was covered with the usual forest of gigantic trees, broken occasionally with a patch of jungle. The undergrowth was composed largely of thorn bushes, which were exceedingly troublesome, on account of the irritation the thorns caused to the cattle. In places it was necessary to clear our passage with an axe, and in consequence of the delays this caused we did not advance more than nine or ten miles. We were quite out of sight of the river Menam, but could see southwards for about seven miles. This was almost the first time since we have been in the country that such an extensive view over the country could be obtained. The landscape was not very attractive, there being little to catch the eye save a monotonous level swamp covered with thorn bushes and the dark forest in the background. A village was visible, however, and, had it been possible, we should have preferred to reach it before halting.

As it was five miles off, this was out of the question.

For the last fifty or sixty miles of our journey we have seen no pea-fowl, and very few pheasants. Parrots and monkeys abound in infinitely greater numbers than any other members of animated nature; and near the water there are large flocks of flamingoes, ducks, storks, snipe, herons, ibises, and bitterns. We have also seen some beautiful species of the kingfisher family; but these are scarce.

Throughout the night we were pestered intolerably with mosquitos, nor are we altogether left at peace by these bloodthirsty little wretches during the day-time, though the gnats are then our chief enemies. Once again this night we witnessed the gloriously beautiful sight produced by myriads of fire-flies on the trees.

JAN. 29.— Passed through the village spoken of last night. It is surrounded by boggy ground where large quantities of rice are grown. Great numbers of fowl and pigs were running about in the streets, and the place appeared to be thickly populated. When passing out of the village a dog ran out of one of the huts and bit one of our attendants in the calf of the leg. The man struck at the dog and killed it, upon which the owner of the animal came out in a great rage, and refusing to accept payment for the damage done, followed us for nearly a mile on the road, heaping all sorts of abuse upon our heads. This is the second squabble we have been so unfortunate as to have with natives of this part of the country.

Three other small hamlets were passed during the day; but as they did not lie in our road they were not entered. We met with several of the inhabitants: some of them at work felling timber, others collecting wild honey. The gutta-percha tree, as well as teak, banyans, and many other fine trees, are very abundant; and we saw great quantities of pepper growing wild. Here we also noticed, for the first time, trees covered with the celebrated lac, which forms such a considerable article of commerce in Europe. It is well known that it is formed through an insect, *coccus laccæ*, piercing the branches, when a sort of gum exudes and hardens. The branches bearing it are called "stick-lac," and look like rough sticks of glue of a reddish hue.

JAN. 30.—After a tedious march of sixteen miles over a country, sometimes boggy and covered with jungle and thorn bushes, at others almost impassable on account of the luxuriant forest growth, we arrived in sight of the gilded domes and minarets of Yuthia, or Siam, the former capital of the country. It was four o'clock in the afternoon before we reached the city, having marched at least twenty-four miles since starting in the morning.

The city of Yuthia, or Siam, as it was formerly called, is built partly upon an arm of the Menam, and partly upon a large island formed by the delta of that river. Like Pegu it has been destroyed by the Burmese, and like that city, it is partly in ruins. In fact, it is quite a decayed place, with little trade, except amongst its own inhabitants and such natives as resort to it for articles not procurable at places farther in the interior of the country. When we entered the city, we found stalls in all the principal streets, and large quantities of merchandise spread out upon cloths upon the ground. There is always great bustle in an Indian city, and Yuthia is no exception to the rule. Natives of all grades and castes crowd the streets, and it is impossible to move very quickly, however anxious you may be to do so. But people who travel anywhere in Southern Asia must never be in a hurry, that is, if you wish to preserve your equanimity. If you want your coat brushed, you must do it yourself (not a pleasant job in a warm climate), or wait your servant's time. If you want the man who runs your errands to make haste, he will obey your wish or will not—just as he takes it into his head. And you must employ a man for each distinct business. If you want your cook to fetch you anything he won't do it, and if you ask the man who washes your clothes to make your bed, he will say—" No, sahib. Me not bed-maker ; me washer-man." But mind you, if you give these rascals extra pay they will do anything—even eat pork. But I am digressing.

We at first thought of procuring lodgings in the city; but the noise and bustle was so great, and the whole appearance of the place so far from enticing, that we altered our intention, and passing out at the south gate pitched our tent under the city walls near a grove of sago palms.

We saw nothing at Yuthia particularly worthy of note, except a sort of dramatic entertainment. The city is not well built, and though some of the houses have three stories, the majority are low (or raised slightly on short piles), and there is plenty of filth about them.

The people themselves are cleanly, well-behaved, and orderly in their transactions. There are many temples and pagodas in the city, but more in the forests around it. The Chinese have several joss-houses, into which strangers can get without difficulty by paying a trifle to the keeper of the doors. However, there is nothing to see save a few hideous idols, one of which was evidently intended to represent an ass.

The dramatic entertainment alluded to above, consisted of a puppet show, in which the figures were made to go through certain parts, something like our Punch and Judy; but, notwithstanding Angbang's endeavours to explain the plot of the piece, we failed to understand it very clearly. It was a love story, and the persons represented were supposed to be of royal rank. What difficulties came in the way of the union of the lovesmitten young people I could not comprehend; but it would seem that papa had decided objections, which, of course, were ultimately transformed into a most beneficent anxiety to see the dusky couple happy in the bonds of matrimonial felicity.

Judging from the excited and boisterous mirth of the crowd, some of the characters must have been very funny in their sayings, and it was rather annoying to us not to be able to understand the pith of Siamese wit. The entertainment was given in the open air, and the figures were well got up, and cleverly worked. After the performance the cup was brought round amongst the crowd, and the donations appeared to be liberal.

We could form no idea of the population of Yuthia; but probably it is not under 40,000 persons, of whom a great number are, perhaps, only temporary residents. The surface of the Menam for a mile above and below the city is covered with floating raft-houses.

After resting a day, we recommenced our journey on the 1st of February, and our progress was much accelerated by having a made road upon which to travel. It is true the road was not one of the best, for it was soft and full of holes; but it took us only about one half the time to perform our day's march of sixteen miles, that it would had we been compelled to cross the rough and boggy country—for much of the region lying be-between Yuthia and Bangkok is morass. This, I think, is owing to the lowness of the banks of the river, so that in the rainy season, thousands of square miles are laid under water.

We saw fields of rice here of hundreds of acres in extent, with numerous flocks of the rice-bird hovering about it, and doubtless doing great damage, since many men, women, and boys were striving to frighten them away, by shouting and waving linen scarves in the air. We also met with a few odd patches of pepper under cultivation, and in one village that we passed through, some scores of Chinese were preparing sago.

This is one of the prettiest parts of the country we have seen : for cultivated land is pleasantly intermixed with patches of forest and groves of feathery palms, and villages, picturesque pagodas, and low houses are frequently met with. In some places we appear to excite great astonishment, in others scarcely any notice it taken of us.

FEB. 2.—The country is in most places fairly peopled; but we passed through a tract of forest extending for ten miles or so, where monkeys and parrots were numerous, and upon making a search we found some small antelopes, four of which we shot. When within sight of the river—which is here quite a mile broad—we saw several fleets of boats and rafts floating down the stream.

FEB. 3.—The heat to-day was great, and Mr. Grant suffered much from it. We halted after marching eight miles or so, and waited for the evening. Thermometer in the shade 104°. Mosquitos and gnats provoked us almost to madness. They even set at defiance the tobacco smoke, which we had generally found efficacious to drive them away. Mr. Grant, who was too ill to smoke, had his eyes bunged up; and we were compelled to keep a man constantly fanning him. The oxen were so tormented that one ox broke loose, and two hours were lost in capturing it.

A little before four o'clock in the afternoon we made a fresh start, and in an hour came in sight of the gilded minarets of Bangkok, and the floating houses on the river; but we did not reach the outskirts of the city until seven o'clock. Angbang had been sent forward to procure quarters for us, and he had been successful. He had taken a large empty house that had formerly been occupied by a native merchant. It was falling to decay; but was pleasantly situated near the confines of the city, and answered our purpose very well; moreover, a large garden attached to it, well supplied with gourds, fruits, &c., was an additional attraction. But we only passed one night in it; for the next day we met with an Englishman, Mr. Fletcher, who was a civil engineer, and had resided at Bangkok for about ten months. He kindly invited us to reside with him during our stay there, an invitation that we gladly accepted, still keeping on our own house or bungalow (if I may use that term in this part of India) for the use of our attendants. We soon found that there were several other Englishmen sojourning in the city, as well as one or two other Europeans, so that we had no lack of society, and altogether passed our time very comfortably here; and Mr. Grant, having perfect rest, and plenty of good nursing, regained his health and strength rapidly, and in a fortnight appeared to have thoroughly recovered.

I am not able to say anything new about Bangkok, and I shall not entertain the reader by repeating in my poor style what others have described so graphically. It is well known that nearly one half of the city is built upon floating bamboo rafts, which are moored in streets in the Menam. The ships which trade to Bangkok sail up the river, and anchor amongst the houses; and as many of the store-houses are erected upon rafts, this gives great facility for loading and unloading the vessels.

The houses are built of bamboo, rattans, palm-trees, &c., formed into a sort of lattice-work, with verandahs in front, and are both pretty and neat in appearance. The temples are numerous and magnificent: but similar to those seen in other parts of the country, and already described. The city of Bangkok covers an immense area, both on the banks of the river and on the water itself. The population amounts to nearly half a million.

Entirely fresh arrangements were now made as to our future proceedings. I was determined to visit the Malay Peninsula; and Captain

Lacy, after due consideration, decided to accompany me. Mr. Grant declined to take part in this fresh expedition, on the ground that he did not think his health would bear the renewed exertion of travelling; and accordingly we paid off all the servants except Laoo and Akbar Nanee, whom myself and Lacy still retained as personal attendants. Mr. Grant undertook to see these discharged men back to Rangoon, to which place we, of course, paid for their passage on board of a merchant steamer then lying in the river. We had some difficulty in finding a customer for our oxen, but the horses were disposed of for nearly double what we had originally given for them. Such of our goods, also, as we were not likely to want or could not take with us, found a ready market here, and fetched (as do all European articles) a high price.

On the 24th of February Mr. Grant and the servants sailed for Rangoon, where it was understood he should be rejoined by Captain Lacy when our proposed second journey was concluded.

CHAPTER XII.

Preparations for our expedition to Malaya.—Sail for Patani.—The ship's crew.—Duration of our voyage.—Patani and its inhabitants.—Trade of Patani.—We land.—Character of the country.—Pass a night in a native hut.—Villages and cultivated ground. — Singular appearance of the forest.—Large snake. — Wasp-like fly.—Gloom of the forest.—Rivulet.—Slow rate of progress.—Exceedingly dense forest.—Rest and sleep.—Our discomforts.

AFTER the departure of Mr. Grant we began to make active preparations for our second expedition, which was one of no little difficulty and danger. The journey would have, of course, to be performed on foot, and to take any amount of baggage or stores was out of the question, as we well knew from report that the country was of a most impenetrable character. With regard to servants for the conveyance of such articles as it was necessary to take with us, we hired two Chinamen who understood English; and these, with Laoo and Akbar, were all the attendants we deemed necessary, as the smaller the party, under the circumstances, the better.

After a great deal of consideration, and some consultation with Mr. Fletcher, we decided that our starting-point should be the city of Patani, a seaport on the north-east coast of the Malay Peninsula, with which considerable trade was carried on by the Siamese. This place was easy of access; for Siamese craft were continually sailing backwards and forwards, as well as Malay proas, &c., and on the 2nd of March, 1870, we embarked upon a vessel belonging to some Bangkok merchants. She was called the *Pujahtah*, and was a small, bulky-looking ship, manned by seventeen seamen, viz., ten Chinese seamen, one Malay, four Siamese, a German sailor who acted as mate, and the captain, also a German. Neither of these Germans were properly qualified to work a ship, having both been merely common seamen; but they had been in their present employment for several years, and had, so far, contrived to escape accidents. Many foreigners are employed by the Siamese to work their vessels, and so convinced are they of the superiority of European mariners, that they will give the charge of their ships to any man who can read the compass; nevertheless, I believe wrecks and other accidents are not so frequent as one would be led to suppose by this fact.

The distance between Bangkok and Patani is

only about five hundred miles, yet it took us eight days to reach the place. We did not reach the mouth of the Menam until the morning of the 3rd of March, and it was evening on the 10th when we arrived off Patani. Although the city is said to contain more than a hundred thousand inhabitants, we could scarcely see a light; but many noises, such as men shouting, dogs barking, and gongs or bells tolling, reached our ears.

At daybreak the city had a pretty effect, as seen from our anchorage. The houses and huts were half-hid from view by the foliage of palms and other trees; and though the city covered an immense extent of ground, it contained few buildings of great size, and I believe no stone or brick buildings at all; but as we did not enter the place I cannot speak positively. Trees were planted in great profusion amongst the houses, and with most charming effect. It is a Malay city, and I believe there are never any permanent European residents residing there. Its trade is very great, carried on principally with other Malay cities on the east coast — with Cochin-China, Cambodja, Siam, and through Siam with China. It is also visited by small craft from all these places, including many junks from China, though the chief trade with the latter country is, as I have said, carried on through Siam. The articles exported and imported are multitudinous, and many of them are such as would not find a market in any European country except as objects of curiosity. The chief and most valuable exports are gold, precious stones (principally diamonds), ivory, areca, vegetable dyes, cinnamon, pepper, cloves, cotton, indigo, various fancy woods, edible nests, birds' feathers (for China), lûche de mer, &c., and many articles used only by the natives on various parts of the coast, and too trifling to be mentioned. The imports consist largely of European goods, especially arms and cutlery; also of linen, fancy prints, gunpowder, combs, looking-glasses, cooking utensils, &c. Pins and needles are much sought after by the Malay merchants of Patani.

About ten o'clock on the morning of the 11th

March we landed, taking with us the Malay seaman from the *Pujahtah*, whose engagement with the German captain terminated here, he having only been employed for the voyage to and from Bangkok. This man's name was Saja, and he was especially serviceable to us on account of his having a sufficient knowledge of the English language to make himself understood, and could thus act as an interpreter between ourselves and his countrymen.

We proceeded on our journey at once, passing through the western suburbs of the city. The streets were full of Malays, Chinamen, and other natives of Southern Asia; and the noise and babbling was very great. Scarcely any women were seen in the crowd; and no domestic animals of any kind except dogs were observed. But there are plenty of fowls here, and they are of immense size.

Proceeding due south we found the country well cultivated, rice being the only grain grown; but there were plantations of areca, cocoa-nuts, indigo, pepper, cloves, and cotton. The villages and hamlets were so numerous, that we were never out of sight of one before we were in view of another. The country was undulating, and so thickly timbered that we could never see more than two miles ahead. Groves of trees were left unfelled between each field, and in the fields also. There were no fences or ditches around the fields, and the roads were merely footpaths, worn by the constant traffic of the labourers.

The weather was close, and the heat great (102° in the shade), and about mid-day we were compelled to halt. Resuming our journey in the afternoon, we made about twelve miles, and then turned into a village for the night. We were received into a hut occupied by three men, seven women, and four children. The three men appeared to be joint owners of the hut—a miserable shanty, about twenty feet square, and full of filth—but we could not make sure about the relation of the women to the men. Polygamy exists in this country, and it is probable that each woman was a wife of one or other of the men. There was only one apartment in the hut, and we all slept together on mats spread over the floor. Neither was there any furniture in the place, except hunting, cooking, and agricultural tools and utensils, all more or less of the rudest manufacture.

In the morning we offered these people four annas, Indian currency, for the accommodation we had received. They took it, apparently understanding the value of the money, and well satisfied with the amount of the reward.

In the distance of five miles we passed six villages, some of them lying a mile or two out of our road on either hand. The ground about and between them was cultivated; but the only productions we could see were rice and cocoa-nuts, and some small patches of pepper. These cultivated tracts ceased quite suddenly, and we came to a dense forest of trees, as gigantic as those seen in Siam, and even more thickly interlaced with creepers, parasites, and other plants of the same nature, insomuch that we found it impossible to penetrate into its depths, and were compelled to skirt along it in a westerly direction, in the hope of finding some break in this barrier. After the lapse of more than an hour we came to a broken tract of country, with hills from fifty or sixty to three hundred feet high, all thickly covered with timber; but we contrived to push in amongst the trees here, and laboriously work our way southwards.

The growth of the trees in these forests was rather singular. The branches shot out from the trunks in a sort of curve, like a bent bow; so that whichever way you looked you seemed to be glancing down a series of leafy tunnels, many of them crossed from side to side with a network of creepers so symmetrical in pattern that it appeared like the work of human hands. So many were the impediments in this forest tract that we could not advance more than a mile an hour, if so far; but it was extremely difficult to make any estimate of the distance actually travelled, on account of the slowness of our advance, and the total absence of any data to guide us in our calculations. We had probably not penetrated farther into the forest than three or four miles when we were compelled to halt for the night, it being then seven o'clock in the evening.

Before lighting our watch-fire, we cleared a few square yards of undergrowth, in order that there might be no danger of setting fire to the forest, and in so doing disturbed a large snake seven feet in length. One of the Chinamen disabled it by splitting its skull with an axe. It was apparently a species of boa-constrictor. The colour of the body was a dingy, yellowish grey, and along the back were markings of a chestnut colour. It continued to writhe for many hours after its head was chopped off.

We did not see many birds in these forests, except parrots, which were numerous enough. Monkeys were plentiful in the tree-tops, and the ground swarmed with small reptiles and insects. Five different kinds of lizards were noticed—one of them a pretty little creature of a golden-green colour. Of the insects the most annoying was the never-failing mosquito, and the most singular a small long-bodied fly. This fly was about the size of a wasp, in shape something like that insect, but more elongated in the body. The colour of the body was a bright ultramarine blue, with white bands; and the wings had a bluish tinge. From the rear of the abdomen hung two long filaments, an inch and a half in length, which gave the fly the appearance when flying of a gnat. It appeared to feed on carrion: for the body of the dead snake was covered with them in the morning, and small holes eaten into the flesh. We also saw it feeding on a dead lizard. Their bite was as painful as that of the mosquito, but they were not so pertinaciously tormenting as that insect.

MARCH 13. — Want of water obliged us to start very early; but our progress was provokingly slow. The density of the foliage overhead was so great as to nearly exclude the daylight, and it was scarcely possible to tell the time without putting the watch close to our eyes. The chattering and screaming of the monkeys and parrots created quite a hubbub above; but they were hid from view amongst the leaves.

Wending our way amidst the trees, and crushing through the underwood, was not only laborious work, but it increased our thirst so much that about eleven o'clock, after seven hours' exertion, we were completely exhausted. But we could not halt for rest long. Our sufferings from want of water were intolerable, and we were obliged to push on in search of it. It was nearly four o'clock in the afternoon before we came to a narrow rivulet, over which we could jump with ease. There was scarcely a foot of water in it, but it supplied all our wants, though we should have liked to have taken a bath—one of the greatest luxuries in a warm climate.

This tiny stream seemed to wend its way through the forest with many windings, and its course in our opinion was north-east; though, owing to the impenetrable nature of the forest, we could not ascertain the direction in which it ran with any degree of certainty. No fish could be found in it—not even those of the smallest kind, which are seldom absent from the smallest Asiatic streams and rivers. This was possibly attributable to the almost total exclusion of light, for the trees interlaced their branches above, and this part of the forest was as gloomy as any other we had passed through.

We encamped for the night near this rivulet. The whole distance that we had made during the day could not have been more than seven or eight miles, though we had been hard at work for upwards of ten hours.

MARCH 14.—As we advanced the forest became more impenetrable. After cutting and pushing our way through the undergrowth—which in most places was fifteen or sixteen feet in height—for five hours, we could not have covered a greater distance than two miles. We were then brought to a dead halt by the thickest and most impenetrable mass of vegetation I have ever seen in any of my wanderings. It was useless striving to force a passage through it. We made the attempt; but every pace had to be cleared with the axe, and in half an hour we had not got fifty yards.

Under these circumstances we had no alternative but to change our route, and we worked our way in a north-east direction back to the stream mentioned above. It was evening before we had accomplished this, and so great was the gloom of the forest, that, although it must still have been tolerably light since the time showed it was about sunset, it was so dark where we were that we could scarcely distinguish one another. With the greatest difficulty we cleared a space sufficiently large to enable us to light a small fire; but that there was great danger in this may be judged from the fact that the bushes in the neighbourhood caught fire and gave us some trouble. Of course had the flames extended to the trees a fearful conflagration would have been the result, in which we should undoubtedly have perished, since we could not move out of the way except at the very slowest pace. We therefore put our fire out, and, lying on the ground round the trunk of a huge tree, were soon in a sound sleep. The indulgent reader will excuse me if I go rather out of my way to make a remark upon sleep. The sweetest and most refreshing sleep I have ever enjoyed has been when I was in positions that most persons would think in the highest degree uncomfortable and perilous. The exertions of a hard day's march make a man oblivious to all danger and discomfort, and the damp ground is to him as great a luxury as a feather bed to the languid idler. The happiest days of my life have been spent in the depths of an Asiatic forest. I had then no care or thought for the future. My heart and mind were free from passions and troubles of all kinds, for there were no objects to excite them. The marvellous beauties and wonderful contrivances of Nature, which were constantly, and with a never ending change, coming under my observance, made my life a continual feast and a frequent occurrence of a spice of danger prevented monotony. It is true I sometimes longed for home; but I now much oftener long to feel the weight of a rifle across my shoulder, and enjoy that free care-for-nought sort of feeling that possessed my mind when marching with a firm steady step across the plains, or forcing my way through the grand old forests of the far East.

MARCH 15.— We tried a fresh mode of making an advance to-day. It was to march down the course of the stream—in the water I mean. I have already said that the depth of the rivulet did not exceed a foot, and although there was another foot of mud, and marching in its weedy bed was laborious work, we got along much faster than when cutting our way through the undergrowth. In some places the stream was nearly blocked with fallen trees, masses of aquatic plants, &c., and we had often to stop to make our way through the tunnel of vegetation; but on the whole we made quite two miles an hour. The course of the stream now appeared to be almost due east; but the windings were so numerous that in following it fourteen miles we did not, I should think, advance eastward more than five or six. In this distance its width and depth were scarcely perceptibly increased. We halted for the day about four o'clock in the afternoon, being very wet and weary; but we succeeded in making a small fire without danger of igniting the neighbouring brushwood, and soon dried our clothing.

CHAPTER XIII.

Continuation of our journey through dense forests.—Gigantic fungi.—Snakes.—Birds' nests.—Exclusion of the sun's rays from these forests.—Our progress southwards.—Pass the night in a hollow tree.—Terrific storm.—Vividness of the lightning.—The two Chinamen leave us.—Their probable fate.—Suffer from thirst.—Difficulties of our passage through the forest.—Intense darkness.—Stream found.—Large baboons.—Hunger and thirst.—Pleasing circumstance.—Springs and pools of water.—Little change in the character of the forest.—Dine off serpents' flesh.—Increased difficulties of our journey.—High trees and monkeys.—Reduced to eat small birds.—Elephant shot.—Beneficial effects of the excitement.

MARCH 16.—We continued pushing our way down the stream for about twelve miles, when the depth had increased to nearly two feet, and in some places three or four feet, which compelled us to leave its bed.

We could nowhere form any idea of the height of the trees in these forests, for the mass of foliage above our heads was so dense that we could only see upwards a few feet. From the sounds of the chattering monkeys and screaming parrots, we were, however, convinced that their height in most places was very great. The trees that had decayed with age had not room to fall; and we saw many of them caught in the boughs of other trees, and inclining at dangerous angles; those that were very rotten threatening every instant to crush their way down amidst the undergrowth. Many of the trunks of both living and dead trees were thirty and forty feet in circumference. On those that were decayed gigantic fungi grew, five or six feet in diameter, of a pale pink and yellowish hue, and emitting when broken a highly offensive odour. Few flowers were seen here, though some of the shrubs of the undergrowth and a few of the trees bore blossoms; but not sufficiently remarkable for colour and shape to call for particular description.

Parrots and monkeys, as I have several times mentioned, were heard in the tree-tops; but we saw none. Neither were any other animals met with. The only creatures possessing life that we saw were lizards, frogs in the stream, a few small birds ranging in size from the bulk of a sparrow to that of a thrush, and insects. In crushing through the brushwood, we also disturbed numerous snakes, most of them of small size. One species was prettily variegated with black and white; its length being a foot or fifteen inches.

Although so few birds were seen, we found several nests. One was skilfully hid in a mass of creepers, and only discovered by accident. It was constructed with vegetable fibres in a beautiful symmetrical shape, and lined with what we felt pretty sure was elephant hair.* There were five eggs in the nest, which were a pale blue in colour covered with brown, black, and purple zigzag markings. Another nest that we found was built entirely of the hair of some animal, apparently of the feline order from its softness, and contained seven eggs, pure white in colour, faintly spotted with red.

The rays of the sun cannot penetrate into the depths of these forests. We knew that it must be shining brightly in the heavens above; but we had only twilight, and could see no object distinctly that was at a greater distance than four or five yards: indeed we seemed to be living in a region of perpetual evening, for we had just about as much light as is usual in this country at eight o'clock at night.

The atmosphere was warm and close, and

* The body of the elephant is sparsely covered with coarse hair.

though the sighing of the wind in the tree-tops was nearly constantly audible, we never felt the least breeze below. When taking active exercise, such as marching or clearing a way through the underwood, we suffered considerably from want of air, experiencing an uncomfortable difficulty in breathing, such as is felt in a close, warm room.

MARCH 17.—We again attempted to march southwards, and this time with some success, though our progress was tediously slow, averaging perhaps a mile an hour, not more. The excessive hard work—additionally onerous on account of the packages of provisions and other stores we were carrying with us—was beginning to tell seriously upon all of us. We had lost flesh and strength during our late exertions, and after six or seven hours' exertion felt quite exhausted. We were obliged to halt frequently and for long intervals; and were further weakened by want of a sufficient quantity of food; for we were compelled to be very economical in this respect, our supplies being limited. We had hoped to find game to furnish us with fresh meat; but hitherto we had not met with any wild animals save monkeys, and these latter, though eatable and even palatable, were out of sight in the tops of the trees, and could not be shot.

We passed the night in the hollowed trunk of a rotten tree, which would have accommodated a party twice as numerous as ours. Often have I slept in a similar billet, for the huge hollow trees found in all Indian forests provide excellent shelter from the dews, which often fall so thickly as to wet one through as if a heavy shower of rain had fallen.

Shortly after midnight we had a tremendous storm of thunder and lightning, the lightning shining with great brilliancy, even in the depths of this gloomy forest; and we could easily imagine how blinding it must have been in an unsheltered spot. The claps of thunder were appalling, the very earth seeming to quake at each report. At intervals there was a lull, when a strong wind appeared to be blowing, the trees rustling with a moaning, mournful sound. Occasionally the terrified birds and monkeys chattered in a low tone, and about three o'clock in the morning we ourselves were terrified by the electric fluid striking a tree near to us. The noise was deafening, and the smell of scorched wood and sulphurous odours nearly suffocating. For the instant that the forest was illuminated by this thunder-bolt, the sight was awfully grand. The leaves, berries, and runners of the creepers were visible much more distinctly than during the day-time, and the whole mass of luxuriant foliage appeared to be enveloped in the most brilliant fire. From the sounds amongst the leaves overhead, we fancied that a little rain fell; but none of the drops reached us. About four o'clock the storm ceased, and an hour later we were on the march.

MARCH 18.—From five o'clock in the morning till seven at night we were, with the exception of a few intervals for rest, working our way through the forest, the character of which is in nowise changed. Myself and

Captain Lacy agreed that in that space of time we had not got over more than three or four miles of ground, our course being south by west. Thoroughly exhausted, we threw ourselves on the ground with our blankets wrapped round us, and slept until the first rays of gloomy light appeared the following morning.

MARCH 19.—While we were preparing to resume our journey, the two Chinamen, Yang-li and Shu-anno, began to mutiny, refusing to proceed any farther, and demanding that we should turn back towards Patani immediately. Of course we refused positively, and one of the men became so insolent that Lacy knocked him down. We could not, however, reduce these fellows to obedience, and they declared they would not advance another step. They seized on a portion of the provisions and attempted to turn back with it. A revolver pointed at their heads compelled them to drop the provisions, but we could not, of course, put any restraint upon their liberty without resorting to unjustifiable means, and they left us, declaring their intention of going back to Patani. For half an hour we could hear them breaking through the brushwood, and talking to each other in a loud tone of voice; but these sounds gradually died away as distance increased between us. We never heard or saw anything more of these two Chinamen. We halted for about three hours, in the hope that they would alter their minds and come back; but they did not, and we resumed our journey. In consequence of this diminution in our numbers, we were under the necessity of loading ourselves with an extra burden; and some of our stores had also to be abandoned. A quantity of shot, two canisters of powder, one hundred rounds of rifle ammunition, a cooking kettle, six pounds of biscuit, and a tin of preserved meat were left in a hollow tree, so that if we were compelled to retreat we might have a chance of recovering our property uninjured by exposure to the changes of the weather. This was a serious loss to us, especially as we were short of provisions.

The disaffection was confined to the two Chinamen. Laoo and Akbar shared all our hardships with great patience; and the Malay sailor, Saja, was a quiet, obedient man, seldom speaking unless spoken to, and never complaining or making any observation about the hardness of his fare.

Our party, reduced to five in number, and having an extra burden amongst them, got along more slowly. We certainly did not travel more than three miles during the day, and perhaps a much less distance. Our fatigue was very great, as besides exerting great strength to force our way through the tangled mass of creepers and undergrowth, we were almost continually using the axe; so that when we had lain down a few minutes for rest we became quite stiff and sore. In making our way through these forests, we were obliged constantly to have recourse to the compass for guidance.

When we halted for the night, we fired several shots, and shouted loudly at short intervals, to attract the attention of the absent

Chinamen, in case they should be trying to make their way back to us. But no answering shout greeted our ears, and I very much fear that these men met with a dreadful fate. They may possibly have found their way back to Patani; but it is far more probable that they perished of hunger before they reached the outskirts of the forest.

MARCH 20.—From eight o'clock in the morning till six at night we were continuously working our way through the forest. The water we carried with us was exhausted, and we suffered extreme thirst. Each man had a wooden keg slung across his shoulder, capable of containing two quarts of liquid. In these warm climates, especially when engaged in active work, a man requires at least four quarts of drink per day. We had been obliged to make two quarts for each man last *three days*; so that some idea of our terrible plight may be conceived. We did indeed obtain a little moisture by cutting some parasitical vines, which yielded a yellowish fluid that was in a great measure satisfying and even strengthening;

but it took hours to collect a pint of this liquid. A kind of red berry grew amongst the underwood, and, being assured by the Malay, Saja, that they were not poisonous, we chewed them constantly for the sake of the moisture they contained.

A new trouble also came upon us. The edges of our axes were so blunted by constant use, that we were compelled to exert additional force to cut away the bushes and tangled plants. This delayed us so much that we did not advance more than five miles throughout the day, notwithstanding our extra exertions.

During the night the darkness was intense, and the heat hardly endurable. The lightning was almost continuous; but there was no thunder. In the intervals between the flashes of light, we could not even see each other's outline. Our thirst was so tormenting that could we have seen our way we should have moved off in search of water.

MARCH 21.—The dim light began to shine, or rather glimmer, down upon us between three and four o'clock, and we commenced our day's labour, being almost too ill and exhausted to move.

How far we advanced in the next five hours it is quite impossible to tell: probably not two miles. But, to our extreme joy, we then came to a stream about thirty or forty feet wide, and containing four feet of water. It required great self-control on the part of Lacy and myself to refrain from drinking an excessive quantity of water. We could not restrain our attendants, and they all three drank more than their stomachs would contain.

While suffering from thirst we had felt no desire for food, and had eaten but little; but now we were all ravenously hungry, and I served out about a pound and a half of biscuit to each man, and divided the contents of a tin of preserved meat amongst us. Towards night a monkey was seen above our heads, and brought down by Captain Lacy. It provided us with what we thought a delicious supper.

MARCH 22.—Of course the stream was easily fordable, and we crossed it about six o'clock in the morning. No fish could be seen in it, and above its bed the trees met and interlaced their branches in a dark, leafy arch, so that not a glimpse of the sky could be obtained. Indeed, from the moment we entered this gloomy forest we have not seen the least patch of the blue heavens above us, and there is something in our monotonous position that is causing us to feel dreadfully dull and melancholy at this continued imprisonment amongst a never ending thicket of trees.

MARCH 23.—We were compelled to use all the water we had brought with us from the stream. We imagine we have covered six miles of ground this day, and perhaps about the same yesterday. Our provisions are getting so short that we are obliged to place ourselves upon a very scanty allowance.

While crushing through the undergrowth we surprised two large baboons, apparently a male and female. They were between four and five feet in height, and when disturbed pulled themselves up into the trees with great rapidity. The colour of the hair on their bodies was black, but about the crown and back of the head of a reddish rust colour.

MARCH 24.—Water was plentiful to-day, for two brooks were found within a few miles of each other. Neither of them was of greater depth than a few inches, and their breadth was not more than four or five yards. We were so fortunate as to shoot two monkeys, and strengthened with their meat and the abundance of water, we succeeded in covering about eight miles. We fancied that the forest in places was rather less dense, a circumstance that spurred us on to renewed exertion.

MARCH 25.—Five miles at the most was the distance got over to-day. The thermometer registered 107° in the shade in this gloomy region; so it may easily be imagined that we suffered no little inconvenience from the heat. Our fatigue and weakness were so great that we were under the necessity of halting every hour or so.

MARCH 26.—No drink to-day except the juice of vines and berries. No idea of the distance traversed, but certainly not more than a few miles. We keep a due south course. The character of the ground up to this time has been undulating; it is now hilly, which makes marching much more laborious. We can form no calculation of the height of the hills, as our view of them is entirely hid by the trees, and we only know that we are ascending them by the sharp angle of the ground under our feet. Our provisions are now reduced to eight pounds of biscuit. Matters wore a dark aspect, and death by starvation or thirst seems by no means improbable.

We saw another pair of large apes to-day. The female had a young one in her arms, which clung round her neck when she climbed a tree to escape from us. We did not attack these creatures, as they were too human-like in appearance for us to think of making a meal off their flesh.

MARCH 27.—Several pleasing circumstances occurred to-day. Shortly after we had started from our halting-place, half dead with thirst, we came to a small break in the forest, and obtained a glimpse of the clear blue sky over

18—2

our heads. The sun was shining down brightly, and for a time we were quite dazzled with the unusual light. This break in the density of the forest was caused by a large mass of rock, from which three springs of beautifully clear water sprang, and emptied themselves into a large pool at its base. On the margin of this pool, which was oval in shape and about two hundred yards in circumference, we discovered the foot-marks of some animals of the deer kind; and our hopes of obtaining a supply of flesh were raised so high that we remained here all day confident of getting a shot towards evening. But we were disappointed. No deer or other animals came near the water.

On the east side the pool had an outlet—a small rivulet running eastward through the forest. The three springs spoken of above were situated at a height of about four feet from the surface of the pool, the water gushing out from the rock with considerable force. They were not more than a yard apart.

MARCH 28.—Continuing our course south, we found little change in the appearance of the forest. We constantly met with the same kinds of gigantic trees, and the same scarcely penetrable undergrowth, and in the space of ten hours did not advance more than six or seven miles. I do not describe minutely our daily experiences, as there is a monotony in them which I fear must be wearisome to the reader. I record only the leading and most noteworthy facts. At the conclusion of this day we had only three small biscuits left.

MARCH 29.—We found water to-day; but suffered the pangs of hunger so severely, that we were compelled to shoot the few small birds we saw for the sake of the scanty meal they afforded us. We only obtained seven of these little birds, four of which were no bigger than sparrows.

MARCH 30. — Want forced us to put up with very loathsome fare. We killed and cooked a large serpent, five feet in length. It was fat and well tasted; but under any other circumstances I should probably have turned from such food with the greatest disgust. We struck a stream to-day, the course of which was south-east. For the sake of having a constant supply of water we pushed along its banks, and occasionally where the water was shallow marched in its bed. In this way we made about ten miles in nine hours' marching, with a few short intervals for rest. This was about the best day's work we have done since entering the forest. Throughout the night thunder and lightning very severe.

MARCH 31.—Continued to move south-east, following the stream. Suffered most acutely from hunger. We were very glad to eat the berries which we found, and the flesh of two or three small snakes. A few birds were also shot; but the scarcity of all sorts of animal life in these forests is remarkable. We do not now often hear the screaming of parrots and chattering of monkeys.

APRIL 1.—We had the good fortune to see and shoot three monkeys this morning; and later in the day a fourth was obtained. The forest is becoming more open, and in places we catch a glimpse of the sky. The trees are of tremendous height — considerably more than two hundred feet. We saw several small colonies of monkeys near the tops; but they were far out of effective range of shot, and were too lively in their movements for good rifle practice. Two of the four mentioned above were, however, killed with bullets. We saw some footmarks of deer near the water, and attempted to stalk the animals, but failed.

APRIL 2.—The course of the stream inclined so much to the east that we could no longer follow it. It was now thirty or forty yards broad, and rather deep, but we did not take any measurement of its depth. We made a direct turn to the west, our intention being to cross the Peninsula to the west coast, and make our way to Province Wellesley as speedily as possible: for the difficulties and sufferings we had endured had sickened us of this country, especially as we had obtained literally no sport.

To-day again we suffered severely from want of food. Only two monkeys and seven or eight small birds were shot, and we were compelled to eke out our scanty meals with such snakes as we could capture. The country is hilly, and though still densely clothed with forests of gigantic trees, not so impenetrable as hitherto. We can see the sky in most places—a sight that is quite new to us. We contrived, in spite of our weakness and miserable fare, to advance fully ten miles in the course of the day.

APRIL 3.—Our march this day was about eight miles, and would have been longer, but that we had the fortune to fall in with a herd of elephants. Notwithstanding my resolution upon a former occasion to take no part in the slaughter of these sagacious animals, hunger overcame all my scruples, and I fired the first shot.

The elephants had taken very little notice of our approach, and we got to within twenty paces of them before delivering our fire. We both aimed at one beast, and when the poor creature felt itself struck, it screamed as if much terrified; and two of its companions placing their shoulders against it, one on either side, attempted to help it away. We had to follow pretty fast to keep up with them, and several times nearly lost sight of the herd amongst the trees. Whenever we could get near enough, we blazed away at the wounded beast; and probably because we could not get a fair aim at any vital part, expended nearly forty rounds of ammunition before it fell. It then required another shot or two to finish it off. The rest of the herd continued their flight after the fall of their comrade, and we let them go in peace, being quite satisfied with our success.

It is surprising what a beneficial effect this little adventure had upon us. The dull, melancholy, hopeless feeling that the monotonous gloom of the forest had engendered, vanished before the excitement of the moment, and when partaking of our supper of elephant-flesh we were quite cheerful. New hope took possession of our breasts, and we lay down to sleep in a more comfortable state of mind than we had enjoyed for a week or two past.

CHAPTER XIV.

The forest less dense.—A herd of elephants seen.—Longer march than usual.—Small pool of water.—Two deer obtained.—Our view of the surrounding country limited.—Handsome parrot.—Trees met with here.—Spring.—Tiring detours.—Our bed.—Decide to make for Province Wellesley.—Chain of mountains in sight.—Flights of birds going southwards.—Halt on summit of hills.—Discovery of tree-huts of wild men.—Thorn creepers.—Wild men.—Their appearance and manners.—A girl captured.—The tree-huts.—Articles found in them.—Description of our captive.—Small river.—Deer and antelope shot.—Guard kept during the night.

APRIL 4.—We left the huge carcass of the elephant about eight o'clock this morning, taking with us as much of the flesh as we could carry conveniently. We had no salt with which to cure it; but had exposed it to the rays of the sun until quite dry, and hoped it would keep as long as we should want it to.

The forest more open than we had seen it at all before. In some few places there were glades two or three hundred yards in extent; but occasionally the forest was so dense as to be almost impassable. The majority of the trees are of very great height. Monkeys and parrots harbour in them, but are not numerous, and few other birds are seen. A herd of elephants was seen early in the afternoon, and we passed quite close to them, but did not molest them.

By dint of considerable exertion we managed

to cover about thirteen or fourteen miles of ground, much of which was very hilly. This long march exhausted us so much that we did not resume our journey until the middle of the following day. Our sufferings through want of water were again intense, and when on the 5th we discovered a small pool of brackish water, we were scarcely able to walk.

This pool was deep, and about a hundred yards across. Its shape was nearly circular, and as we could find no means by which it was fed, we came to the conclusion that it had been filled during the rainy season, and not yet evaporated. The water was palatable enough to men in our condition; but it possessed a peculiar, sickly taste, that certainly would have led us to avoid it in disgust at ordinary times. It would seem that wild animals had no antipathy to it, for traces of deer were found all round the margin, and at sunset we shot two of a very pretty and graceful species, and weighing, at a rough guess, about sixty or seventy pounds each. No circumstance that had occurred since we had been in the country gave us more pleasure than the shooting of these deer. For not only did they furnish us with a much needed supply of good fresh meat, but we were also encouraged to hope that they were the harbingers of a tract of country better stocked with game than that which we had passed through.

APRIL 6.—We found the forest now so open as to offer little impediment to our progress; still the face of the country was covered with it, and in consequence our view of the surrounding landscape was very limited. Ranges of hills, varying much in elevation, ran from about north-west to south-east; the highest of these being, perhaps, five or six hundred feet. In places the ascent was steep enough to cause us to feel rather tremulous about the knees; but this was due, undoubtedly, in a great measure, to our weak condition.

During the day we saw five herds of elephants, numbering from twenty to forty per herd. Besides these we saw a solitary elephant quietly browsing amongst the trees. We did not disturb any of them, having no need of meat. No other animals of any description were found except, indeed, a few monkeys. A parrot that was shot is worthy of note, as neither myself nor Captain Lacy had ever seen one like it before, and it may probably be unknown to European naturalists. The colour of the back, head, wings, and tail, was a deep green; the wings were marked slightly near the edges with crimson. The breast was yellow, each feather being slightly edged with red. The beak was larger than is usual in most parrots.

The areca, teak, banyan, and some other trees common to India were seen occasionally; but by far the greater number of trees met with were of species which we are unable to name. Many of them, however, were of kinds frequently seen in Burmah and Siam. Palms of different sorts were plentiful, and we obtained a great many cocoa-nuts, which afforded a delicious refreshment — the more acceptable as water was scarce.

About three o'clock in the afternoon we altered our course again to due south, marching in the wooded valley between two ranges of hills. We continued our march till eight o'clock, in the hope of meeting with water. We were disappointed; but cocoa-nuts were so abundant that we had no difficulty in satisfying our thirst. It is worthy of remark that no cocoa-nut trees were seen in the dense forest-covered region from which we appear now, happily, to have escaped.

APRIL 7.—Three hours after starting we discovered several springs of water, the sources of rivulets running west by south. One welled up from the earth in the valley—the others (four in number) sprang from the rocky sides of the hills. They all yielded deliciously refreshing water.

Though the forests here were tolerably open, and the undergrowth not at all troublesome, we were compelled to make so many detours to avoid dense patches of vegetation, and met with so many impediments in the shape of rocky, broken, and hilly ground, that though we marched diligently for ten hours we did not cover more than sixteen miles in a line direct south; but had probably tramped twenty-four, reckoning the windings. We were very tired when a halt was called, and slept soundly during the night.

Our bed was invariably the earth, our pillows the packages we carried with us. When we could find a commodious hollow tree, that appeared to be free from dangerous insects, such as centipedes, scorpions, snakes, &c., we usually chose it as our resting-place; at other times we were content with arranging a bed of grass, &c., on the bare earth, over which we spread our blankets, and then wrapped in our cloaks would obtain sleep that was generally both sound and refreshing. During the whole time of our stay in this wild country, we had to content ourselves with billets of this kind.

APRIL 8.—Before resuming our journey this morning we held a consultation whether we should continue to move southwards, or make for the nearest port on the coast, with a view of giving up our explorations of the country. We were rather undecided on this point; but determined at length that we would march southwards one day more, and if the country did not afford us some encouragement to proceed, in the shape of a tolerably plentiful supply of water and game, we would cross over to Province Wellesley without further delay.

This resolution formed, we marched from our ground about ten o'clock, finding the country much the same in character as that already described. When our view of the surrounding country was not intercepted by tall trees or hills, we could see lofty ranges to the westward, rising ridge above ridge. Through a glass these mountains (or at least those nearest to us) appeared to be covered to their summits with trees.

Soon after mid-day we saw two storks flying south by east, and shortly afterwards a flock of some small birds passed over our heads, going in the same direction. These latter birds, we fancied, were ibises, and thought it likely that there was some large body of water to the southeast. We accordingly altered our course in the hope of finding it.

We found fewer impediments in our way than

usual, and by two o'clock in the afternoon had marched about twelve miles. We then halted on the summit of a hill, which, according to a small aneroid we had with us, we thought to be about five hundred and fifty feet above sea level. Far in the valley beneath us, to the southward, we were rejoiced with the sight of the largest stream we had yet seen in the country. We judged it to be about eight miles distant, and only a few glimpses of it could be obtained when there were breaks in the forest which hid its course. While searching the country in the neighbourhood of this river, through our glasses, our notice was attracted by what seemed to be some enormous birds' nests in the trees. The size of these nests was prodigious, yet they were not placed at a very great height from the ground, nor in the tallest trees. The number of them was seven, but we concluded there were others not visible from our position. We were puzzled to think what bird could construct nests of this size, for they appeared from our point of view to be as big as tolerably-sized huts, and much the shape of roughly-constructed wigwams. While we were still speculating, the difficulty was solved. A large ape was observed to leave one of the nests and descend to the ground ; and he was soon followed by eight or nine others, who all walked about erect like men. We watched them for a long time, and saw them picking berries or something else of a similar kind, from the bushes. Their actions were most human-like. They walked about exactly like men, and even appeared to be talking to each other. Several of them climbed the cocoa-palms in search of the nuts ; but they did not display that activity in ascending which distinguishes most of the ape tribe. Their every motion was human in the extreme.

Greatly astonished, we commenced to descend into the valley about four o'clock, and make our way towards the river. The ground was rough, and overgrown with a sort of creeping thorn plant, which retarded our progress so much that we were obliged to give up all thoughts of reaching the river that night. These thorn creepers were most troublesome. The thorns found their way through the worn soles of our boots; and our feet and legs were soon full of them; and not only were the pricks painful, but they also caused a considerable amount of inflammation.

APRIL 9.—We were on the move early as we were in want of water. It took us an hour to get over a mile and a half of the thorn-covered ground; but after that we had a tolerably good country covered with forest. A little before seven o'clock we came in sight of the apes' nests. Nine of the apes were on the ground, and remained oblivious of our approach until we were close upon them. I was almost dumbfounded with astonishment when we discovered that these supposed apes were men. There could be no mistake about it. The form of the feet and hands, and the hair of their heads, proved beyond a doubt that they were of the same species as ourselves; but how degenerated! I had heard of the wild men of Malaya, but had not expected to find them in this part of the country, and the sight filled me with the most intense astonishment.

The pitiable objects before us were completely

naked, both men and women. The colour of their skins was very dark, nearly black: indeed, some persons would probably have described them as black men. Their stature was under-sized, the height of the men being about five feet two or three inches, that of the women five feet, or perhaps rather less. Their hair was allowed to grow long, and hung about their heads and necks in a tangled mass of filth; giving them the appearance of having dispropor-tionably large heads. Their limbs and bodies appeared to be smeared with dirt, and their whole appearance was disgusting. In coun-tenance they were not repulsive, though I need scarcely say they were far from good-looking; but their expression was idiotic in the highest degree, and whilst looking at them I could not wonder much that some have classed the most noble of God's creatures with the ape tribe.

So intent were they upon digging up roots of some kind, that, screened by the bushes, we approached to within forty yards of them, and remained watching them for nearly a quarter of an hour before we were discovered. A sneeze from Laoo first attracted their attention. For one instant they stood as if paralysed with astonishment, then, setting up a shrill scream, ran away at a pace that took them out of sight amongst the trees in a minute or two.

The scream alarmed those who were in the hut or nest in the trees, and they commenced to swarm down to the ground like a lot of monkeys. One woman, in her haste, fell a distance of ten or twelve feet, and before she could rise we had hold of her. The rest effected their escape, disappearing in the woods.

The woman we had captured howled most piteously and fought desperately, biting a piece clean out of Akbar's arm. She did not appear to be hurt by her fall; but was evidently terrified to find herself in our clutches. Saja, by our direction, tried to make her comprehend that no injury would be done to her; but we saw at once she did not understand a word he spoke. She was quite a girl, being apparently about seventeen or eighteen years of age. As she continued to struggle violently, and strove hard to use her teeth, we bound my lady hand and foot, but as gently as possible, and did our best to reconcile her to a temporary bondage.

Leaving the three men to guard her and prevent a rescue, we went to examine the nests or tree-huts. They were from thirty to fifty feet from the ground, built in the lower branches of a species of large, wide-spreading tree, in general appearance very much like the oak. Access to them was gained by a number of notches cut in the tree-trunk; but we, being novices in the art of climbing, found it no easy task to ascend. Several times we lost our precarious footing and had narrow escapes of coming headlong to the ground, and when we got amongst the branches, we had to crawl out snake-fashion, to get at the huts, which were the shape of a bee-hive, though rather more pointed at the apex. They were constructed entirely of small branches and twigs tied together at the top and bent round to form the hollow space in the interior. The height of each hut was about six feet; the internal diameter about the same. The entrance was a hole in the side, so small that we could scarcely force our way in. All that we found within the huts was a quantity of leaves, which seemed to serve as a bed; some bones, the remains of a meal; a curious instrument made of bone, and apparently intended to serve as a knife; and a sort of tomahawk, formed by fixing a pointed stone upon a stick. The cordage with which the huts were constructed was made of some tough creeper, and the strands were so loosely twisted together that the least touch parted them. Outside the huts a number of spears were laid amongst the branches of the trees. They consisted merely of long sticks of hard wood sharpened at both ends.

Underneath the trees in which the nests were built, we found the horns of deer and charred bones, proving that these people had been making a meal of animals of this kind. Several fires were still smouldering, and we found roots roasting amongst the embers. The roots that these people had been digging up with sticks when we disturbed them, lay in heaps upon the ground; and were similar to beet-root in appearance, but of a lighter red in colour. The plant which they nourish grows to a height of six or seven feet, and bears a large green, apple-like fruit, of a nauseous taste.

All the time that we had been making these notes, our captive had been alternately crying and screaming, yet we were so anxious to communicate with these strange people that we were unwilling to let her go; being convinced that if we could induce her by kind treatment to be friendly with us, we might easily induce the others to be less shy and fearful of us. With this end in view we unbound her hands and feet, but made her sit upon the ground and kept a sharp watch upon her. She was already less violent in her conduct, and now made no attempts to bite. By-the-by, she had fetched a piece out of Akbar's arm the size of a crown piece, and the wound afterwards festered badly as though it had been inflicted by the foul teeth of a wild beast. By way of amusing her, we gave her a few silver coins and some other trifles to play with. They attracted her attention immediately, and she left off crying to examine them. The silver sixpences, and a few brass buttons that had come off my uniform jacket, especially took her fancy, and she rapidly became reconciled to our society. In the course of two or three hours she had become quite contented, and manifested no desire to make her escape ; but we were much disappointed to find that her companions showed no signs of returning, though possibly they were hiding in the woods near at hand and waiting for our departure.

Meantime we had been down to the river distant about half a mile, and found that it was from sixty to eighty yards wide. Its course was from north-west to south-east ; but we could not trace it more than a few hundred yards, either above or below stream. Its banks were clothed on both sides with a thick forest growth, and creepers ran across from tree to tree, forming aërial bridges, over which the monkeys ran with great nimbleness. In many places the trees met over its waters, and where the banks were clear of timber there were abundant traces that it had been burnt down. We saw a great many small fish in the shallow parts of this river.

Finding that the inhabitants of the tree-huts gave no indications of an intention to return to their homes while we remained in the neighbourhood, we gave our captive her liberty, thinking she would go to her people and show them that she had been kindly treated; but when she found that it was not our intention to keep her a prisoner, she evinced no desire to leave us. We tried by signs to make her understand that we wanted her to fetch some of her people, but without success. She chatted incessantly in a rude, guttural language that sounded like a series of grunts, and was evidently vexed that she could not make herself understood. When we cooked a little dried venison she ate her share of it, and fetched some of the roots mentioned above, which she roasted and held out to us. We tried them and found that they had a pleasant mealy taste, and were probably highly nutritious.

To induce these queer people to come back to their huts we removed ourselves to the banks of the river, followed by our ex-captive; and during the afternoon searched amongst the woods near the water for game. A herd of about ninety small deer or antelopes were found grazing amidst a patch of thorn-creepers, of which plant they appeared to be very fond. We fired amongst them, killing two; and at the report of our rifles our savage companion displayed the most abject terror. She screamed with fright, and would have fled had not Lacy caught hold of her. We soon succeeded in pacifying her in some degree; but her teeth chattered and her knees trembled for an hour afterwards, and if in moving our rifles we advanced them near her she cowered behind in great alarm. She examined the deer also, pushing her fingers into the bullet-holes, and uttering exclamations of astonished wonderment.

The deer or antelope (I believe they properly belonged to the latter species) which we had shot were both males, and weighed about eighty pounds each. They had been feeding on the thorn-plant, and their mouths were pricked and bleeding; but animals of the deer kind, and also rhinoceros, seem to be very fond of thorns, and to have no objection to the laceration of the mouth which the spiny food produces.

Evening came on; but none of the wild men made their appearance, and our savage friend made it apparent that she had no intention of leaving us. When we made preparations for passing the night she coolly appropriated one of the blankets, and imitating ourselves wrapt herself in it, and appeared to fully enjoy the luxury.

Not knowing but that a surprise might be attempted, we kept guard in turns all night; and several times heard the wild men prowling about near us. We did not, however, see anything of them, and they made no demonstration of an attack.

CHAPTER XV.

Our captive's appetite.—Succeed in communicating with the wild men.—Their degraded state and morals.—Numbers.—Mode of procuring fire.—Resume our journey.—Our captive anxious to go with us.—Proceed up the river.—More dense forests.—A white peacock.—Appearance of the range.—Pool or lake.—Find a couple of tapirs and shoot one.—Description of the animal.—Valleys with pools.—More tree-huts, and traces of supposed cannibalism.—Country difficult of access.—Another colony of wild men.—Find it impossible to communicate with them.

At daylight on the morning of the 10th April we had breakfast, our savage lady friend displaying a prodigious appetite. She consumed at least ten or twelve pounds of roast deer flesh.

After a bath in the river we went to the tree-huts, which were distant about a mile. As we neared them we observed a large party of the wild men drawn up under the trees. They showed some inclination to fly at first, but our girl ran up to her companions and appeared to explain that we were friendly, upon which they came and surrounded us, staring at ourselves, our arms, and accoutrements with an expression of stupid wonderment.

It was impossible to gaze upon these poor wretches without a feeling of intense pity at their miserable condition. So degraded and abject were they that one might almost be excused for saying they were only one degree removed from the ape tribe. Both men and women were entirely devoid of clothing, and most of the latter betrayed evidences of having been treated with revolting brutality. Their bodies were covered with sores and bruises, and smeared with blood; and even in our presence the men struck them fiercely if they attempted to push too near to us; and the poor girl with whom we had become so friendly kept between myself and Lacy as if she expected violence.

The persons of all these people were disgustingly filthy, and infested with vermin; and not even the rudiments of morality seemed to exist amongst them. Moreover, we had good reason for coming to the conclusion that wedlock, in any form, was not recognised by them; and, indeed, in their manners they were even more degraded and lost to a sense of decency than the lowest orders of the animal creation. It is impossible to say more than this.

The number of these deplorably savage people standing around us was sixty-nine, of whom five were children, two of them being infants at the breast. Forty-eight were women, and sixteen only men, which led us to think that some of the males were absent on a hunting, or some other expedition. Their physique was miserable, the limbs of the men being scarcely larger than those of boys, and the poor women were emaciated to a terrible degree. To convince them of our friendly intentions we gave them the remains of the two deer we had shot yesterday. They lit fires immediately and proceeded to cook the flesh, squatting on the ground until it was done. Their method of procuring fire was by rubbing two pieces of dry rotten wood together till they ignited.

Between nine and ten o'clock we resumed our journey. Our departure was not noticed by the savages. They scarcely even looked round after us; but the girl with whom we had first communicated got up and followed us. We motioned to her to go back, and she in turn tried by gestures to induce us to return to her people; she even caught hold of Lacy by the arm. She had manifested a particular liking for him, and seemed very unwilling to part from him. When she had accompanied us about two miles, finding that we were determined to go on, she suddenly turned back without displaying the least emotion. Once or twice she looked back as if undecided whether to leave us or not; but we hurried on lest she should take it into her head to favour us with her company farther on our journey than would be altogether agreeable. In a few minutes her form was lost amongst the trees.

We marched up the stream—that is in a north-westerly direction, keeping as near its banks as possible; but we were frequently obliged to make wide detours to avoid dense forest patches and marshy ground near the river. Westward, the ranges of hills were fully visible, and as we advanced, the country became so elevated that the course of the river was altered, and it now flowed from almost due north. Its breadth at the point where the bend took place was about sixty yards; but a mile higher up it was reduced to thirty, and in fording it we only found four feet of water.

Marching westward, the country rapidly became mountainous, being well covered with forests, inhabited by monkeys, parrots, crows, and pea-fowl. The last named has not been seen in this country before by us; and it is not very plentiful. In addition to these birds, pigeons are very numerous, especially in the hilly tracts; and we shot between thirty and forty as we marched along. In the evening we halted in the midst of a wood which was free from undergrowth, and here we found many deer, in small herds of from a dozen to twenty or thirty each. Three fine bucks were obtained.

APRIL 11.—We were all day forcing our way through a forest tract, almost as dense as that met with at the commencement of our journey. Unlike that dreadful region, however, this country was fairly stocked with game; for, besides a few deer, we saw in the course of the day nearly a hundred elephants, four rhinoceroses, and abundance of monkeys, parrots, pigeons, and other birds. In the tops of the tallest trees a few pea-fowl harboured, and a white one was seen and shot. This was the first time I had seen a white peacock in a wild state.

The distance travelled this day was not more than seven or eight miles, and when we halted for the night we were between five and six hundred feet above sea-level. Westward was a range of lofty mountains, distant about thirty miles. We could trace it north and south for an immense distance, some of the peaks appearing to rise to a great height. The country lying between us and this mountainous range was a succession of hill and valley as far as we could see.

April 12.—In a narrow valley between two low ranges of wooded heights, we discovered a pool or small lake. It was of irregular shape, about a mile and a quarter long, by half a mile wide. We could find no traces of it on the map we had with us, and therefore concluded that it was not a permanent body of water, or had not been previously discovered. Many storks and splendid rose-coloured flamingoes were observed wading about in the lake, and from the distance they could wander from the shore, we perceived that the water was very shallow. These birds were probably in search of frogs and water lizards, as we could find no traces of fish in the water. A thick growth of reeds choked up the south corner, and it was nearly entirely surrounded with a forest of enormous trees. In the mud we saw many traces of elephants, and a herd of these animals was seen in the neighbourhood.

But the principal incident of this day was the discovery of a couple of tapirs, for which this peninsula is so celebrated. They were found about half a mile away from the lake, lying in a patch of tall grass, and apparently fast asleep. When disturbed by our near approach they rose, uttering a low grunting sound, not at all unlike that of a pig, and endeavoured to make their escape. One was shot down before it had got twenty yards, being pierced with three bullets; but the other, though wounded, rushed through the forest, crushing its way amongst the undergrowth. We followed in its wake for nearly a mile, and obtained two shots at it, but it ultimately escaped into a part of the wood so dense and overgrown with creepers that we could not keep up with it, and were obliged to give up the chase.

Returning to the beast we had slain we were informed by our men that after we had left it for dead it had risen and would have escaped had not Akbar put another bullet through its head. It was an extraordinary creature, about the size of a small rhinoceros—that is to say it was just eight feet in length, and about five in height. The shape was also similar to that of a rhinoceros; but it was furnished with a singular proboscis ten inches in length, and terminated by a sort of round knob or fleshy excrescence. The colour of this animal was white, except the head, neck, shoulders, breast, and fore-legs, which were jet black. This gave the animal a most curious appearance, as if a pair of black trousers had been pulled over its fore-legs and fastened about its neck. Its skin was even thicker than that of the rhinoceros, and covered with coarse hairs, black on the black portions of its body and white on the others.

APRIL 13. — In every valley we passed through we found small pools of water, fed by springs, and discharging the superfluous water in tiny rivulets, running for the most part in a south or south by west direction. We found more winged game near these pools than had been seen in any part of the country previously passed through. Flamingoes, storks, and a species of bittern were abundant; and we had capital sport with birds that were more or less good for food; the following bag being made: seventeen pigeons of two varieties, five peacocks, nine pheasants, fifteen ducks of three different varieties, and ten other birds of odd kinds. The pheasants and some of the ducks were birds of extremely beautiful plumage.

Towards mid-day, having advanced about eight miles over country that was in places difficult of access, we came within view of another village of tree-huts, if I may so designate it. Only four of the elevated dwellings were visible; and though we searched the country around carefully with our glasses we could see nothing of the inhabitants. In a couple of hours we arrived under these four huts, and found them exactly the same in construction as those already described. At the foot of the trees were large heaps of bones and filth, amongst which we found what appeared to be the skull of a child. It might have been that of a large monkey; but both Captain Lacy and myself thought it a suspicious circumstance, and felt sure that we were not mistaken. As, however, the skull was mutilated, and the teeth entirely wanting, we could not come to a satisfactory conclusion.

As we had had a fatiguing march of ten miles we halted here; but none of the people came near us. They had possibly seen and heard us shooting, and were terrified at the deadly effects of our weapons. We ascended to the huts, but found literally nothing in them save filth. We kept quiet and tried to hide ourselves during the afternoon, in the hope that some of the people would show themselves, but they did not; and though we kept strict watch throughout the night nothing was heard of them.

APRIL 14.—Again we met with dense patches of forest and jungle, which retarded our progress very much. The hills, which we were continually crossing, were more remakable for steepness than height, few of them being more than four or five hundred feet in elevation. Growing on the sides and summits we found several species of pine-trees, a few specimens being from a hundred and fifty to two hundred feet in height.

Snakes were abundant in this region, some of them six or seven feet in length; but they were inoffensive in so far as they always strove to get out of our way. No large game was seen, but we found traces of elephants. In spite of all drawbacks we covered fully sixteen miles to-day—one of the longest marches we have made in the country.

APRIL 15.—Very stiff and tired; the result of yesterday's prolonged exertion. In consequence we only crossed one range of hills this day, and advanced to the base of the elevated mountains which have been visible during the past week and more. This occupied four hours; the rest of the day was devoted to shooting. Plenty of deer were found in the more open parts of the forest, near the pools and springs. They were shy (probably through being frequently disturbed by the wild men), and we had great difficulty in getting near to them. Of the four we succeeded in killing one was shot running at fifty yards, one running at between three and four hundred yards, and the remaining two standing at distances of three hundred and four hundred and fifty yards respectively. They were small in size, and easily killed by a rifle bullet if fairly hit. A fifth that we fired at had its fore-leg smashed, but it nevertheless got away and we were unable to follow it.

Wandering in the forest we suddenly, and without any previous warning of their proximity, came upon a party of thirty or forty native wild men. They fled upon our approach, but we found no difficulty in keeping them in sight, although we could not overtake them, and chased them for about a mile, when they reached their village, and uttering cries of alarm, the women, as we supposed, for we were not near enough to make sure, came down from their tree-huts and joined them in their flight. One miserable object was a cripple, and tried to make his escape on all-fours, jumping along with great rapidity. He was soon captured, and endeavoured, by a horrible display of facial distortions, to intimidate us from touching him. His limbs were wasted away by rheumatism, or some disease of a similar nature, and he was quite incapable of standing. From constant crawling on his hands and knees, the skin on these parts had become like sole leather, and his nails had been suffered to grow until they had become quite horny like the claws of a beast of prey.

We gave this unhappy creature a few trifling articles which we happened to have about us, and which we thought were likely to attract a savage eye; but he refused to touch them, and was evidently in terror for his safety. Leaving our presents on the ground near him, we proceeded back to our halting-place, distant about three miles. As we passed near the dwellings of these people, we saw that there were fifteen huts—one or two in a tree. The usual heaps of bones and rubbish lay underneath at the foot of the trees, and we found that they had been feeding upon both deer and monkeys, and we also saw the remains of birds, snakes, &c., tending to prove that these wretched people are in the habit of eating whatever they have the fortune to lay hands on.

The next morning we made another attempt to communicate with these savages, and succeeded in surprising them. We arrived under their trees before they became aware of our presence, and though we made every possible demonstration of friendliness, they evinced the wildest terror, and refused to come down from their trees. Some of them seized their spears, or pointed sticks, and made other active preparations for attack or defence; and as we feared they might throw their weapons, we withdrew behind the shelter of the tree-trunks, upon which they commenced to swarm to the ground, men, women, and children, all completely naked, their bodies thickly covered with hair (perhaps the result of exposure to the weather without covering or clothing), giving them a most beast-like appearance. All our efforts to stay the flight of these people were unavailing. As fast as they reached the ground they ran off into the woods, and when once or twice we went out and attempted to approach them, they raised their sticks in a threatening attitude, and we were compelled to retire to prevent a collision. Nothing was seen this morning of the crippled man.

We lay by for a rest the remainder of this day, shooting about the neighbourhood in the evening.

CHAPTER XVI.

Commence ascent of the mountains.—Sides very steep and covered with forests.—Gamboge and pine trees.—Growth of the trees.—Our highest point.—Pigeons.—Dark night.—Sublime scene.—Descend on the west side of the range. Fearful storm.—Quantity of game.—Party of natives.—Their weapons.—A nearly white tapir shot.—Use of the proboscis.—Hilly district.—Retarded by denseness of the forest.—Follow the course of a stream.—A large python. Description of the river.—Reach the sea-shore.—Purchase a prah at a Malay hamlet, and set sail for Penang.—Arrive at Georgetown.—Conclusion.

APRIL 17; being Easter Sunday.—We commenced to ascend the mountainous range westward, between four and five o'clock in the morning. The day was warm (102°), and we found the ascent rather distressing. We had chosen, as we thought, the lowest and most accessible portion of the range; but it was very steep, nevertheless, and the ground so broken and rough that it was with the utmost difficulty that we succeeded in dragging our baggage along with us. By ten o'clock, according to a rough calculation of our elevation, made by means of the aneroid, we had only ascended about 2,000 feet. We then halted for rest, and owing to the great heat (which at seven o'clock had risen to 110° in the shade), could not resume our laborious ascent until five o'clock in the afternoon.

Up to 2,000 feet we found the sides of these

mountains thickly covered with forest; but after that elevation was attained the trees began to be scattered, and the forest to appear only in patches. The majority of the trees after 3,000 feet were pines; but at this height we found the gamboge tree. The gamboge resin was issuing from the trunks, and dropping to the ground; it was also clotted in large masses on the bark, but the excessive heat had made these masses soft and of the consistence of pitch.

Some of the pine trees were of very pretty and graceful shape and foliage, and of species that I had not observed in any other country. The height of them was very great, and some that we measured were eight feet in diameter a little above the ground. Monkeys and parrots were noticed as high up these mountains as about 2,500 feet, and pigeons were found on their summits.

The steepness of our ascent was extraordinary, and such as I have never experienced in other mountains. In places the ground was covered with fallen trees, whose weight, coupled with the great inclination at which they grew, had torn them up by the roots. In other places the forest trees had a most remarkable inclination to the eastward; and sometimes the face of the mountain was so exceedingly steep that no trees could maintain a hold upon it, and such spots were covered with a growth of coarse grass, creepers, dwarfed pines and jungle plants. Some idea of the difficulty of the ascent may be obtained by the length of time it consumed. The first 2,000 feet was attained in five hours, which was partly owing to the denseness of the forest: we arrived on the summit in three hours more, the total height above sea-level being rather over 4,000 feet.

It was now eight in the evening, and the sun had set; 'but there was twilight sufficient to show us an immense tract of country, stretching away on the east and west sides of us. Northwest the country appeared to be mountainous; but it was too late in the evening for us to be able to ascertain its characteristics.

While the twilight lasted, we had some excellent pigeon shooting; for the trees here were not more than eighty or a hundred feet high, and the birds were in consequence not able to get out of range of our fowling-pieces. We knocked over between three and four dozen.

The night was intensely dark, and, what in these eastern lands is remarkable, there was no lightning, yet throughout the night the thermometer stood at $80°$ to $82°$. We supposed that the heat during the day in the plains had been tremendous.

At sunrise on the 18th, the sight was heavenly in its sublimity. I dare not attempt to describe it. The sun rose red and fiery, and revealed to our eyes scores of miles of splendid forests, relieved by romantic-looking mountain ranges, lit up with a radiance which persons unacquainted with the brilliant charms of tropical countries can have no conception of. To me the view was so glorious and delightful, that I felt it was worth a life-time of labour to enjoy it.

We commenced to descend on the west side at six o'clock, and found the face of the mountain not quite so steep as on the east; but clothed like it with forest, which was very dense near the base. The fauna met with consisted of pigeons and mosquitos at our greatest elevation; parrots commenced at about 2,800 feet, monkeys at 2,400 feet, some hawks at 2,000, small birds, finches, lizards, and small snakes at 1,500; boa constrictors (not exceeding five or six feet in length) at 1,000, and from 1,000 feet downwards we found the forest very full of all sorts of small birds, monkeys, and reptiles.

We arrived at the foot of the mountains soon after ten o'clock, and at that time found the heat so excessive that we could not advance across the plain. It was, indeed, extraordinarily hot; and at noon the thermometer stood at 119°. About four in the afternoon, a frightful thunderstorm commenced. Trees were riven to atoms by the electric fluid, and several partially burnt monkeys and birds fell near us. A deluge of rain fell, and as we were unable to find effectual shelter, we were soon drenched to the skin. This storm lasted for three hours, and we were prevented from making any farther movement that day.

APRIL 19.—Started westward about five o'clock. Country mostly covered with dense forest; but some open tracts and small plains. We found mangosteens and other fruits in great abundance, and met with no less than five herds of deer, besides a herd of between sixty and seventy elephants. Many of the deer could have been shot down, but we contented ourselves with the slaughter of two to supply our present wants. We marched about fourteen miles this day.

APRIL 20.—Between ten and eleven o'clock we discovered a party of human beings, distant about a mile or so. Through our glasses we could see that ten or a dozen of them were sitting round a fire and eating. A few others were moving about in the jungle near them; but we could not see any of their dwellings or nests in the trees near at hand.

All savages are very quick of eye, and these people must have seen us, especially as we did not attempt to conceal ourselves, hoping that if we did not appear before them too suddenly they would be more disposed to communicate with us than those we had met with hitherto ; but they showed no signs of noticing us until we were within two hundred yards of them, when they rose up, collected together in a crowd, and appeared to await our approach. As soon, however, as we got a hundred yards nearer, they bolted in a body, and every man of them was out of sight in five minutes. Half an hour later we passed their village. It consisted of five huts built in the trees, and seven hovels erected on the ground. They were built of branches like those described in a former chapter, but were overlaid with deer-skins.

In the interior of one of the huts were a number of short thick sticks, intended apparently as missile weapons. Several of them had traces of blood and feathers adhering to them, as if they had been used for knocking down birds. The only other articles found were a number of sharpened stones, serving the purposes of knives. Heaps of grass in most of the huts served the purposes of beds.

We had plenty of water to-day from the pools collected during the recent storm. The rain had been sufficiently heavy to lay some low-lying districts under water. Two herds of deer, and two of elephants, were seen, besides great numbers of birds, consisting principally of pheasants, pigeons, a species of quail—which is found also in Hindoostan, and a fine pea-fowl. These latter, it should have been mentioned, are not of the common Indian kind; but of the same species as the Javanese pea-fowl. This day we also saw a tapir, but at such a distance that we could not get a shot at it.

APRIL 21.—Another tapir was seen early this morning, and a second about noon, which was shot. This specimen was less in size than the one killed on a former occasion, and it was nearly entirely white, only the fore-legs, shoulders, and head being black. It is difficult to comprehend the use of the curious proboscis with which the animal is furnished. It is not long enough to be of use to it in pulling down the branches of trees upon which it feeds, and it is not used in drinking like the trunk of the elephant.

The distance travelled this day was about twelve miles over a country sometimes thickly covered with forest, and sometimes open, with only a sprinkling of trees. It was hilly, some of the elevations being eight or nine hundred feet above sea-level. We halted at night on the outskirts of an extensive forest.

APRIL 22.—In order to keep our course due west, with the object of reaching the coast, we were compelled to plunge into the depths of the forest near which we had passed the night. We found it nearly impenetrable, and though we made most strenuous exertions to cover as much ground as possible, the distance actually travelled in ten hours could not have been more than as many miles. We were compelled to halt for a rest frequently, and suffered from the scarcity of water. None was met with during the day, and at night the limited supply which we carried with us was exhausted.

APRIL 23.—The need of finding water speedily and the sufferings we experienced from want of it, induced us to resume our journey at three o'clock in the morning. In four hours we made about five miles, and got clear of the forest. An hour later discovered a stream on our right, and after a couple of hours' rest proceeded to follow its course westward. It was not more than thirty yards wide; but eight miles further on, where we halted for the day, its width had increased to fifty yards. Numerous pheasants of handsome plumage inhabited the woods near its banks, and we had good sport with them and the pigeons.

APRIL 24.—Constant and excessive fatigue, accompanied with a diet consisting entirely of meat and water, had reduced us to an uncomfortable plight, and we were anxious to bring our ramblings to an end for a time, in order to recruit our exhausted frames. We accordingly made a forced march of about eighteen miles this day, choosing a course parallel to and about a couple of miles from the river. The country was partly level, partly hilly or undulating, and covered with timber of large growth. The distance accomplished will prove that we did not meet with many impediments to our progress; but in places the jungle and undergrowth was troublesome and caused us delay. In one of the forest districts we destroyed a large boa or python, eighteen feet in length. It was coiled round the trunk of a young teak tree, and upon receiving a couple of bullets through the head, lashed out furiously with its tail. The Malay Saja, seizing his opportunity, closed with it, and hacked it nearly to pieces with an axe. It was of a grey or dark drab colour above, yellowish beneath, and prettily marked in a network pattern with black and brown.

APRIL 25.—The river has now increased in breadth to about eighty yards. There are many fish of considerable size in its waters, and water-fowl of the stork, bittern, snipe, and duck families are numerous. We also disturbed a small herd of elephants, which were disporting themselves in the river; and as we were in need of meat we shot one of the beasts. Nine bullets brought it to the ground, after it had made desperate efforts to escape from us. No other four-footed game was seen; but we came across several large apes, and monkeys innumerable.

The obstacles met with to-day were many, and our progress bad. The ground on the right bank of the river appearing to be the best adapted for travelling, we forded across, finding about five feet of water in mid-stream, though in most places the river was much deeper.

April 26.—Forcing our way all day through dense forest. No food but dried elephants' flesh and a few pigeons; fare that has become quite loathsome to us.

April 27.—To our great joy we came in sight of the sea about two o'clock in the afternoon, and at eight encamped on its shores. The forest and a thick growth of luxuriant vegetation ran down as far as high water-mark; and the river, a few hundred yards above its mouth was nearly a quarter of a mile broad.

We concluded that at this point we were only about forty or fifty miles south of Province Wellesley, and hoped to be able to march that distance in three or four days.

April 28.—While marching along the shore we observed a steam vessel far out at sea, apparently working her way northward, and probably making for Penang. Between nine and ten o'clock we reached a Malay hamlet, consisting of thirteen huts. Through Saja, we were enabled to communicate with these people, and purchase a quantity of rice, and a prah. We embarked on board the latter, with the intention of running along the coast till we came to Penang. The wind was dead against us, and we were obliged to keep constantly at the oars. As night came on we landed, and the next morning continued our voyage. We came in sight of Penang before mid-day; and at six o'clock in the evening arrived at Georgetown.

Here my narrative must end. Captain Lacy soon left by the mail for Rangoon, taking, by his own desire, the Malay Saja with him. I myself remained some time longer at Georgetown, and ultimately took passage back to Calcutta, bringing my travels, for a time, to a conclusion.

Though greatly reduced by a lengthened period of hard marching, and want of proper lodging and food, it is worthy of remark that I was in excellent health at the end of our journey, nor did I afterwards suffer any inconvenience owing to the arduous tramp of which the foregoing pages give a narration.

THE END.

www.ingramcontent.com/pod-product-compliance
Lightning Source LLC
Chambersburg PA
CBHW031854220426
43663CB00006B/623